VANCOUVER CANUCKS

THE FIRST TWENTY YEARS

WRITTEN BY

NORM JEWISON

FEATURING PHOTOGRAPHS BY

BILL CUNNINGHAM

POLESTAR

BOOK PUBLISHERS

To the fans of the Vancouver
Canucks, whose undying
enthusiasm, loyalty and support
make them the very best in the
National Hockey League.

Published by
Polestar Press Ltd., #3 - 373 Baker Street, Nelson, B.C. V1L 4H6
(604) 354-4482

Distributed by
Raincoast Books, 112 East 3rd Street, Vancouver, B.C. V5T 1C8
(604) 873-6581

Canadian Cataloguing in Publication Data

Jewison, Norm.
The Vancouver Canucks

ISBN 0-919591-49-3

1. Vancouver Canucks (Hockey team) — History.
I. Title.
GV848.V35J49 1990 796.962'64'0971133 C90-091589-7

Acknowledgements
We would like to thank the following for the use of their photographs in this book:
Bill Cunningham
Wayne Leidenfrost
Jack Murray
Derrik Murray
Chris Bickford
Kent Kallberg
B.C. Sports Hall of Fame & Museum

Cover illustration by Glen Green

Book design by Jim Brennan

Printed in Canada

Cover
Members of the Canuck Dream Team, as chosen by fans,
(clockwise from top): Harold Snepts, Stan Smyl, Don Lever,
Paul Reinhart, Thomas Gradin, Richard Brodeur.

CONTENTS

BEFORE THE NHL CAME TO TOWN

The date: mid-February, 1966. The place: the St. Regis Hotel, New York City. The event: the NHL Board of Governors' meeting to supervise doubling the League in size from six to 12 teams. An anxious group of Vancouver investors waits in the wings to learn of the NHL's decision. But when the dust had settled, the Canucks' group was left in the lurch, clutching its $2 million entry fee, passed over in favour of six U.S. cities that were awarded franchises.

Howls of outrage were heard locally and nation-wide as Canadians saw their beloved sport slipping away from them south of the border. The sentiment was kept at a fever pitch until 1969 when the NHL finally relented, granting franchises #13 and #14 to Buffalo and Vancouver. In the interim, the entry fee had jumped to $6 million, creating a financial dilemma for the original applicants. The problem was eventually solved, however, and on May 22, 1970, the National Hockey League finally counted Vancouver among its lodge members.

Today, the franchise has progressed from the bouncing baby of the '70s, past the trials of teenhood in the '80s, to a fresh new decade full of hope, promise and ... a truckload of fond memories. It is these memories of the Canucks' first 20 years that we will chronicle in this book, primarily those as seen through the eyes of indefatigable team photographer, Bill Cunningham.

Two men who were largely responsible for putting Vancouver on the hockey map. In the early days (circa 1915) it was Fred (Cyclone) Taylor ... much later, Orland Kurtenbach was a Western League Canuck star before becoming the NHL Canucks' first captain and MVP in 1970.

This had to be one of the first hockey games ever played in Vancouver as the early 1900s townfolk play on a frozen Trout Lake.

But before we deal with the two decades in question, it must be pointed out that hockey enjoyed a rich tradition in Vancouver well over half a century before the current Canucks played their first NHL game.

Prior to 1927, the trustees of the Stanley Cup would accept bonafide challenges to the National Hockey Association (forerunner of the NHL) winner. In 1915, a tough Ottawa Senators club defeated the Montreal Wanderers to win the Cup on March 13 and promptly received a challenge from the champions of the Pacific Coast Hockey Association, the Vancouver Millionaires.

The Senators boarded a train in the nation's capital and set out for the first-ever Stanley Cup series to be played west of Winnipeg. And the locals were ready for them. Led by the legendary Fred (Cyclone) Taylor, Frank Nighbor and Mickey Mackay, the Millionaires delighted a wildly-cheering, jam-packed crowd of 7,000 at the old Denman Street Arena by trouncing their eastern visitors 6-2. Two days later Ottawa bounced back to lead 2-0 after one period, but Vancouver poured it on after that to win handily, 8-3. The third and final game was a shambles for the Senators as the Millionaires skated wild, pummeling the defending champs 12-3 and leaving little doubt that the brand of hockey being played on the West Coast was far superior to that in the east.

The Millionaires were Stanley Cup winners and were awarded the heady total of $300 per man for their efforts. The Senators slunk home with $200 apiece and

Great hockey and the Stanley Cup came to Vancouver long ago, although most of us weren't around when this team won the Cup in 1915.

L to R: K. Mallin, F.J. Nighbor, F.W. Taylor, F.A. Patrick, H. Lehman, L.T. Cook, D. McKay, R. Stanley, T.J. Seaborn. Centre, S. Griffis.

This 1967 publicity shot illustrates the many and varied forms of entertainment Pacific Coliseum would stage once opened in January, 1968.

The Pacific Coliseum, home of the Canucks, in its infant stage (1967). (Note Callister Park Stadium, upper left, now a grassy park.)

The Canucks weren't in the NHL yet when this shot was taken, but NHL hockey was in the Coliseum. Here, the WHL Canucks take on the NHL Los Angeles Kings in exhibition action, Oct. 7, 1969.

Lester Patrick Cup victory jubilation is written all over the faces of these 1969-70 WHL Canucks. From Left to Right: Germain Gagnon, Len Lunde, John Arbour, George Gardner, Ted Taylor, Andy Bathgate.

severely wounded pride. Vancouver's prowess was no fluke as it remained a solid contender, finishing as a Cup finalist five more times over the next nine years.

The Pacific Coast League was listed as "amateur" in 1945 and operated for three years before the Directors voted to professionalize it in 1948. Now known as the Canucks, this team played to packed houses at the old PNE forum for the next 20 years and in the brand-new Pacific Coliseum for their final two Western League seasons. During their WHL tenure, the Canucks captured the Lester Patrick Cup as league champions four times — 1958, '60, '69 and '70.

Many famous NHL players either began or finished their careers in Vancouver. Such notables as Emile Francis, Gump Worsley, Larry Popein, Andy Bathgate and Tony Esposito all played for the Canucks at various points in their careers.

And so it was May 22, 1970 ... just 10 days after Bobby Orr scored his spectacular "airborne" goal to give Boston a Stanley Cup win over St. Louis ... and 20 days after the WHL Canucks captured their last WHL championship ... that the NHL was finally in Vancouver!

The celebrations continued in the dressing room as displayed by (L to R) Murray Hall, Gerry Goyer and Ted Taylor.

The last Western League Canucks team went out with a bang in 1969-70, winning the WHL championship with 102 points and going 8-0-3 in the playoffs to capture the Lester Patrick Cup.

LET'S GET STARTED

1970-71

Now that the Canucks finally had their NHL franchise, the next order of business was to select the players that would make up the team. So 19 days later (June 10), the Canuck contingent — led by Vice President and General Manager Bud Poile and Head Coach Hal Laycoe — joined the rest of the NHL brass in Montreal's Queen Elizabeth Hotel for the annual meetings and drafts.

First order of business for the fledgling Canucks and Sabres was the Expansion Draft, the lottery in which they'd each receive 18 skaters and two goalkeepers in exchange for their $6 million. The existing 12 teams had filed protected lists with the League and Vancouver and Buffalo had to fight over the leftovers. A coin was flipped and the Sabres won the toss, choosing Tom Webster (current L.A. Kings coach) from the Boston Bruins. Canucks countered by picking defenceman Gary Doak from Boston. Vancouver's second selection was Orland Kurtenbach from the New York Rangers, the man who was to be the team's first captain and Most Valuable Player through Canucks' first three years of existence. Then came forward Ray Cullen from Minnesota and fourth choice was a big, hard-nosed defenceman from the Toronto Maple Leafs named Pat Quinn. (The same man now, of course, directs the current Canucks from his office of President and General Manager.)

Vancouver concluded the 18-man portion of the draft by adding forward Garth Rizzuto to their roster from the Chicago Blackhawks. The expansion club was rounded out with the

Here's a piece of history — Canucks' first NHL goal. The date was Oct. 9, 1970. The scorer was defenceman Barry Wilkins (#4) and the goalie was L.A. Kings' Denis DeJordy.

13

Canucks' inaugural NHL team (1970-71). Front Row (L to R): George Gardner, Danny Johnson, Ray Cullen, Lyman D. Walters (Vice President), Orland Kurtenbach, Thomas K. Scallen (President), Gary Doak, Wayne Maki, Dunc Wilson. Second Row (L to R): William Winnett (Vice President), Bud Poile (Vice President & General Manager), Mike Corrigan, John Schella, Barry Wilkins, Charlie Hodge, Poul Popiel, Bobby Schmautz, Garth Rizzuto, Hal Laycoe (Coach), Babe Pratt (Asst. to the Vice President). Back Row (L to R): Greg Douglas (Public Relations Director), Ed Shamlock (Trainer), Andre Boudrias, Rosaire Paiement, Pat Quinn, Dale Tallon, Murray Hall, Ted Taylor, Bill Gray (Trainer), Miles Desharnais (Ticket Manager).

selections of netminders Dunc Wilson from the Philadelphia Flyers and Charlie Hodge from the Montreal Canadiens.

The following day featured the Amateur Draft and, again, the two new teams would have first crack at the available talent. The opening scene will be forever etched in the minds of Vancouver's drafting contingent. NHL President Clarence Campbell was presiding over the proceedings and was set to spin a large "wheel of fortune" which would determine the order of selection. Each GM was to opt for either an even or an odd number at which the wheel would stop. Poile went with even numbers, leaving Buffalo's Punch Imlach with odds. You could have heard a pin drop in the crowded ballroom as Campbell spun the wheel. When it finally came to rest, the League President shouted: "Number two!" Whoops of joy went up from a jubilant Canuck table. But the ecstasy was short-lived.

"Hold on a minute, Mr. Campbell," yelled Imlach. "That's not a two; it's an eleven!" Sure enough, the President had misinterpreted the "II" as a Roman numeral for a two. It was time for the Sabres' table to erupt with joy. Imlach promptly selected Gilbert Perreault and awarded him jersey number 11, which the Buffalo star wore for his entire 17-year career with the Sabres.

The Canucks regained their composure and chose Dale Tallon, a promising 19-year-old from the Toronto

Following the infamous spin of the wheel, Canucks selected Dale Tallon as their first-round draft choice.

Marlboros of the OHA, and a player who could play either forward or defence. Vancouver selected five more players in that draft and then withdrew to contemplate the talent of its fledgling team. Management set up shop at the Pacific Coliseum and busily prepared for Canucks' first training camp which was held that September in Calgary.

Meanwhile, back in Vancouver, fans were champing at the bit in anticipation of Oct. 9, 1970, the night of their home debut. The Canucks would host the Los

The hated stop 'n' starts were all part of
Canucks' first training camp in 1970.

Opening night, Oct. 9, 1970, saw the arrival
of a host of dignitaries such as Premier
W.A.C. Bennett and son Bill, just behind at
left.

Angeles Kings in the only NHL game slated that night. It was truly a momentous occasion in the history of local sport and no instance of pomp and ceremony was spared. The Vancouver Beefeater Band trumpeted in such luminaries as Premier W.A.C. Bennett and his son Bill, NHL President Clarence Campbell, Vancouver Mayor Tom Campbell, Native Chief Dan George, plus a host of other NHL Governors and dignitaries.

After the final speech and formality were out of the way, referee Lloyd Gilmour dropped the puck and game one was underway ... at long last!!!

Everything ran smoothly except for one thing ... the Kings didn't follow the script. After a cautious scoreless first period, L.A.'s Ross Lonsberry scored while Canucks' Mike Corrigan was serving a hooking penalty. And with eight seconds to go in the second frame, Bob Berry tallied another to give the Kings a 2-0 lead. But then, with each team skating five aside, Vancouver

The ever-colourful George Gardner was in goal for Canucks' inaugural game against Los Angeles, Oct. 9, 1970.

Orland Kurtenbach was the cornerstone of the Canuck franchise. He was the team leader both on and off the ice, and earned MVP honours the first three seasons he played.

defenceman Barry Wilkins (who had one prior NHL goal to his credit) took a pass from Len Lunde and fired the puck past L.A. goalie Denis DeJordy. The Canucks were on the board, but it wasn't enough as Barry scored his second of the game against Vancouver netminder George Gardner and the Kings won 3-1.

If nothing else, the Canucks showed that night that they weren't going to be pushed around as both Orland Kurtenbach and Rosaire Paiement engaged Dale Hoganson and Ross Lonsberry in fights, while feisty Pat Quinn drew two minors and a misconduct. And while he didn't make the scoresheet, rookie first round draft pick Dale Tallon fired six shots at DeJordy. And, oh yes, the house was full with 15,564 rabid new fans. The NHL had, indeed, arrived!

On-ice action captures the attention of Pat Quinn (#3), Dale Tallon (#9) and coach Hal Laycoe.

Coach Hal Laycoe and five of his charges appear to be checking out some material for team blazers in this photo from Year One. From left to right are Dale Tallon, Poul Popiel, Laycoe, Wayne Maki, Dunc Wilson and Barry Wilkins.

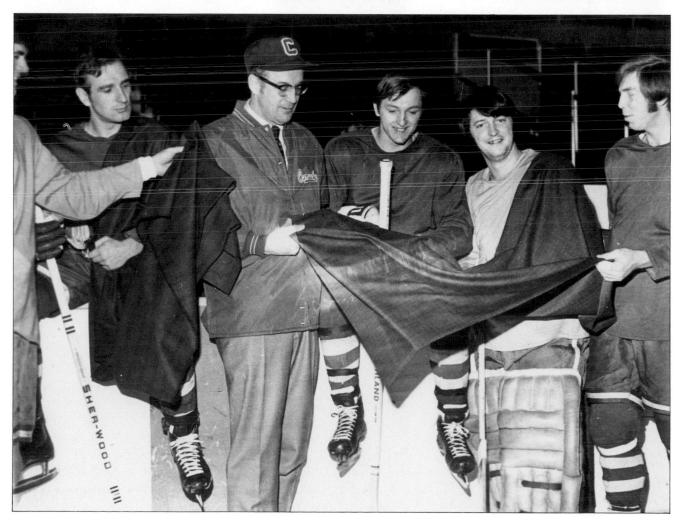

Coach Hal Laycoe guided the Canuck fortunes for the first two years of the franchise's existence, and had 44 wins and 16 ties to his credit.

Murray Hall was nearly 30 years old when he joined the Canucks but tallied 21 goals and 38 assists in his first full NHL season.

Early action from the Pacific Coliseum shows a stern coach Hal Laycoe presiding over defencemen Barry Wilkins (#4), Jocelyn Guevremont (#22) and John Schella (#5).

Early media coverage of the fledgling NHL Canucks was intense. Here, Denny Boyd, Sun Columnist and radio personality, confers with GM Bud Poile.

Canuck play-by-play man Jim Robson conducts one of over a thousand post-game interviews, this one with Murray Hall.

NHL action from 1970-71 included a visit to a Canucks/Canadiens game by Soviet Foreign Minister Andrei Gromyko flanked here by captains Orland Kurtenbach of Vancouver and Henri Richard of Montreal.

Adding flash, dash and crash to the first year Canucks was Rosaire Paiement who led the club in both goals (34) and penalty minutes (152) in 1970-71.

Nothing was as electrifying in Year One as a visit by the fabled Montreal Canadiens. Here, goalie Dunc Wilson thwarts Hab bad-boy John Ferguson.

More '70-71 action involving the Canucks and Canadiens. Hab's Marc Tardif (#11) and Yvan Cournoyer (bottom) prowl the goal area while Canucks defend with goalie Dunc Wilson, defenceman Gary Doak (#2) and forwards Mike Corrigan (#12) and Danny Johnson (#8).

FORMATIVE YEARS

Two days after dropping their home opener 3-1 to the Kings, the Coliseum was once again filled to the rafters as the Canucks hosted the Toronto Maple Leafs, a team many Vancouverites had grown up with, thanks to the legendary Foster Hewitt and Hockey Night in Canada.

This was to be a very different story than Game One. With little Charlie Hodge in goal, the Canucks ran roughshod over the Leafs, building up a 5-0 lead by the nine-minute mark of the third period. Toronto scored three late goals but the locals prevailed 5-3 to register their first of 24 victories in 1970-71, the same number as their expansion cousins, the Sabres. The scrappy Canucks, thin in talent but deep with character, finished sixth in the NHL's East Division, 26 points out of a playoff spot.

Year One, while not fraught with success, was nonetheless memorable in many ways. Goalie George Gardner, who remained in Vancouver after his playing career was over, has these recollections: "That first year here was a fun season. Very few of us had much NHL experience; most of us were fringe players. But we were actually quite a competitive team for an expansion club. We did all right by winning 24 games."

Coach Hal Laycoe, now a realtor in North Vancouver, recalls: "It was an amazing team, really, one that was unusual and unappreciated. To this day, I can recall each and every one of the players. Charlie Hodge was just incredible for us. He'd only played 12 games in each

Andre Boudrias, the man they affectionately called "Superpest" was responsible for a large portion of Canucks' early offensive production as he led the team in scoring four times in the club's first five seasons in the NHL. And though he retired from the Canucks some 14 seasons ago, he remains in fifth place in all-time team scoring with 388 points in 458 games.

Goaltender Charlie Hodge had a winning record with an expansion team, 15-13-5.

Bobby Schmautz was a Canuck fixture for four seasons, scoring 150 points. Then he left for eight years, returning for a last hurrah in 1980-81. All told, he played 285 games for Vancouver, scoring 108 goals and 103 assists. His personal best was 1972-73 when he connected for 38 goals. Included in that total were two four-goal games plus another hat-trick.

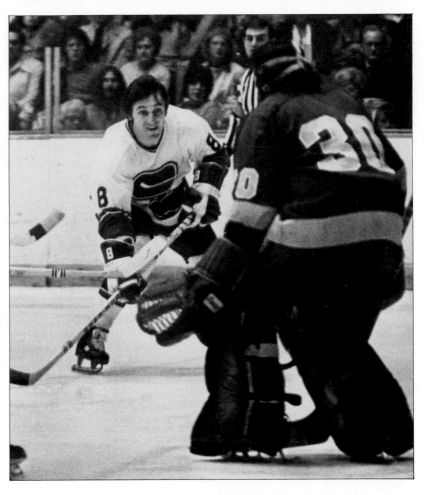

of the previous two seasons, yet he won 15 for us. He had a winning record (15-13-5) for an expansion team. How about that? We had six 20-goal scorers, none of whom had scored that many before in the NHL, and four plus players in the plus/minus column."

Laycoe remembers another momentous occasion. "If there was one game that really launched us into credibility, it was our 5-4 win over Boston, the defending Stanley Cup champions. Rosie Paiement scored four goals in that game and the people just went wild. After that, we sold out all our games and we had a waiting list of over 3,000 for season tickets."

Right winger Bobby Schmautz, the only Canuck ever to register two four-goal games, reminisces about the character of the team. "Hal (Laycoe) and Bud (Poile) did a pretty darn good job of putting that team together, considering what they had to work with. I can't tell you how many goals I had (five) that first year with the Canucks," says Schmautz, now in the roofing business in Portland, Oregon, "but I *can* tell you it was a good, tough team with a lot of character. They were a great bunch of guys on that club ... guys who stood behind one another. And I was proud to be one of them."

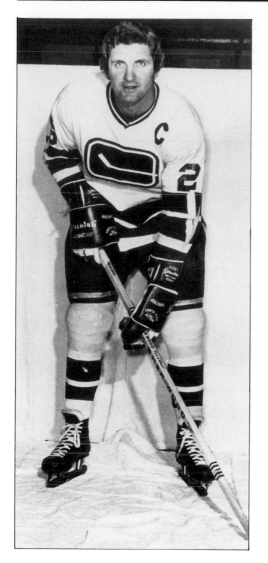

Orland Kurtenbach, the Canucks' big, tough captain, had a world of influence on the fledgling club.

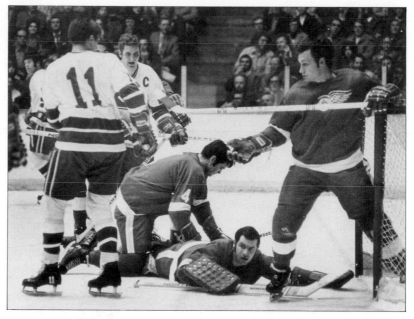

ABOVE RIGHT:

Action was hot and heavy around the Detroit goal in this 1971-72 scene featuring Canucks Orland Kurtenbach (wearing the C) and Wayne Maki (#11). Red Wing defenders are Arnie Brown (#4) and Larry Johnston (leaning on goal), with goalie Andy Brown sprawled on the ice. (The two Browns were not related but Andy was the last NHL netminder not to wear a mask.)

Charlie Hodge recalls some of his teammates. "The younger players, especially Dale Tallon, felt the pressure; Dale was smothered by it. But I came here as a veteran; I was used to it. We weren't all that bad defensively, but we had no big gunners. Basically we relied on Kurt (captain Orland). And when he got hurt after Christmas, we gradually fell out of playoff contention. I remember what a great example Pat Quinn's work ethic was to the other players. He may have been just an adequate player but he was a great person. His character made him a superstar on that team."

Maybe the Canucks didn't have a gunner quite as potent as Boston's Phil Esposito who fired in 76 goals in 1970-71, but Rosie Paiement got the attention of many a goalie that season, too. Given the opportunity at playing regularly for the first time in his career, Paiement wasn't an instant hit. While the fans cheered his hard-nosed play (he led the team with 152 penalty minutes), he didn't get his 20th goal until the Canucks' 57th game. But, in mid-February, he went on a tear, adding 14 more to his totals before the year was over to finish the season with 34.

An eye injury inhibited Paiement the following season, and the lure of the neophyte World Hockey Association was too much for the French-Canadian winger in 1972. "I loved hockey," said Rosie. "But I was always a businessman first. And I was offered a lot more money to play in the WHA. . . . I just couldn't refuse it."

Orland Kurtenbach, who operates a golf driving range in White Rock and also coaches B.C. junior

An early blueline fixture was Tracy Pratt who patrolled the Canuck defence for nearly three seasons. The hard-nosed rearguard was the son of Canucks' goodwill ambassador and Hockey Hall-of-Famer, the late Babe Pratt.

Action from Year Two sees Pat Quinn #3 lugging the puck out of the Canucks' end with Pittsburgh's Syl Apps in pursuit and Jocelyn Guevremont behind him.

hockey, remembers being grateful for the chance to be an NHL regular. "Those early days with the Canucks were the first *real* seasons in my career," says Kurt. "I got a lot of ice time, I was on a regular line, killed penalties and got on the power-play. It was a good hard-working team and we made the opposition pay for what it got."

Pat Quinn was a 26-year-old journeyman defenceman with the Toronto Maple Leafs in 1969-70 when he found out he'd been drafted by the Canucks. "I was delighted," Quinn recalls. "The Leafs were going with kids on defence and I didn't figure in their plans. So it was a new lease on life for me to come out here (Vancouver). I guess the thing that sticks in my mind most about that first year was this: in spite of being a rag-tag, thrown-together group, we all got along famously *and* we were competitive." Quinn, of course, has gone full circle, from Canucks player, to Atlanta player, then to the Flyers and Kings as coach, and finally back to Vancouver as President and General Manager. Along the way, he earned his law degree from the Delaware Law School and University of San Diego.

1971-72

Following the excitement and hoopla which surrounded Year One in the NHL, the Canucks fell on hard times in 1971-72. The raw enthusiasm and adrenalin that had propelled them to 24 wins had dissipated somewhat while the rest of the league

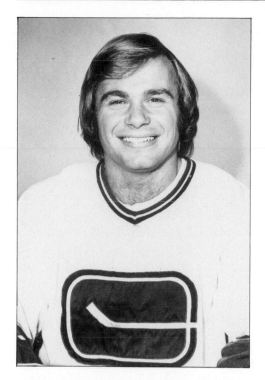

A crowd favourite all the while he was a Canuck, little Bobby Lalonde was literally a buzz-saw on skates. Though he was the league's smallest player at 5'5", 155 lbs., Lalonde was durable enough to play in 353 Canuck games before concluding his NHL career with stops at Atlanta, Boston and Calgary.

members got back to the business of dominating their Expansion partners.

Coach Hal Laycoe's charges were hard-pressed to win 20 games and suffered through 50 losses, both totals being franchise lows and highs. These hardships were not exclusive to Vancouver, however, as its counterpart, Buffalo, won just 16 times that same season. The number of 20-goal scorers dipped from six to four, and many wondered what had gone wrong. Rosaire Paiement, for example, was so perplexed at his drop in production — from 34 goals in '70-71 to just 10 the next season — that he sought the help of renowned hypnotist Reveen! The move backfired as Rosie didn't score again for 17 games.

But on the bright side, several players consistently brought smiles to the faces of their fans. Little Andre Boudrias and captain Orland Kurtenbach tied for the team lead in scoring with 61 points, giving "Boud" a two-year team leading point total of 127, and Kurtenbach the most productive season of his career. First-round draft pick Jocelyn Guevremont, a big defenceman from the Quebec Junior League, finished third in scoring with 13 goals and 38 assists for 51 points. Left winger Wayne Maki continued his solid

Coach Bill McCreary surveys the scene from behind the Canuck bench. McCreary had a brief (41 games) career as Vancouver's third coach in 1973-74.

Happy scene from a 1973-74 press conference shows a smiling new coach Bill McCreary and first-year Canuck goalie Gary Smith. McCreary coached that season only while Smith went on to sparkle in goal 'til the end of 1976-77.

For the first six seasons of their existence, Andre Boudrias was an offensive sparkplug. The little (5'8", 165 lb.) centre scored 388 points in 458 games and is still solidly in fifth place in all-time Canuck scoring. Boudrias was the only four-time winner of the Cyrus McLean Trophy as Canucks' leading scorer.

role begun the year before, tallying 22 goals and 47 points.

Season highlights included the first shutout in club history by goaltender Dunc Wilson, a rare 0-0 tie (the only one ever by the Canucks) against the Toronto Maple Leafs and netminder Bernie Parent. At the other end of the ice, Boudrias recorded the first of his two career hat-tricks when he pumped three goals behind New York Ranger goalie Gilles Villemure in a 5-2 Canuck victory.

These sporadic bright spots got Vancouver no nearer than 32 points from a playoff berth. Their dismal seventh place finish did nothing for Bud Poile's health, either, and shortly after the season was over, the General Manager suffered a health setback. Coach Laycoe was elevated to the post of acting GM and, on May 2, 1972, the Canucks announced they'd hired Vic Stasiuk as their new bench boss.

1972-73

On June 6, 1972, the NHL admitted two more franchises to the fold, the New York Islanders and the Atlanta Flames, bringing total league memberships to 16 clubs. The very next day, the annual amateur draft was held, and Vancouver had third pick over-all. They wasted no time in selecting a young centre from Niagara Falls of the OHA, Don Lever, a player who was to be a Canuck cornerstone for the next eight seasons

Bruin goalie Ed Johnston kicks out an Andre Boudrias shot. Darryl Edestrand checks Boudrias while Bobby Orr prepares to clear the rebound.

Netminder Gary Smith was brilliant in 1974-75, earning six shutouts and back-stopping the team to its first title. Here, he stymies Guy Lafleur with John Grisdale in pursuit.

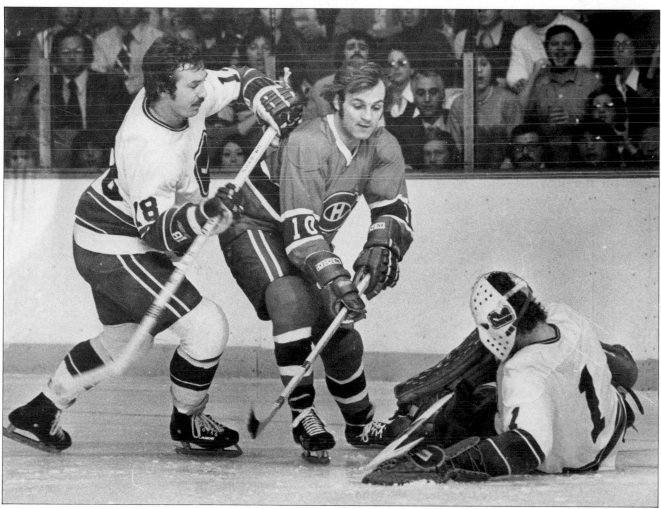

Harold Snepsts as a rookie in 1974.

and who remains in fourth place in all-time team scoring as the current season begins.

That fall, when camp broke in Medicine Hat, Alta., everyone was filled with renewed optimism that this was the year the Canucks would make great strides. And as the erstwhile Andre Boudrias' name was again at or near the top of the team scoring race, a host of new faces made inroads of success. Bobby Schmautz blossomed into a full-fledged NHL'er with a 38-goal, 33-assist performance to beat out Boudrias by a single point. A pair of young French-Canadian centres — Bobby Lalonde and Richard Lemieux — became instant crowd favourites with their dashing style and scoring prowess.

The club registered a record seven hat-tricks (including an amazing pair of four-goal games by Schmautz) and recorded two shutouts. But again, the over-all performance was not enough to make it to post-season competition. On May 14, 1973, team management made a major trade which did not reap immediate dividends, but was to bring eventual unprecedented success down the line: original first-round draft pick Dale Tallon was dealt to Chicago for defenceman Jerry Korab and goaltender Gary Smith.

On June 13, Vic Stasiuk was let go and Bill McCreary became Vancouver's third coach.

1973-74

Canucks' fourth NHL season marked the end of the "first chapter" in the history of the hockey club. Many things happened during this campaign which were to thrust the team into a new era.

Due to illness, GM Bud Poile was forced to cede the reins to Hal Laycoe. And when the club convened in Medicine Hat, Alta. for training camp '73, rookie coach

A couple of heavyweights get set for a classic scrap...Steve Durbano of Pittsburgh and Dave Dunn of the Canucks. Linesmen Swede Knox (L) and Leon Stickle (R) don't appear too anxious to intervene.

Phil (Fox) Maloney coached Canucks to their only division title in 1974-75 and to a second-place finish the following season, the only two times the team finished better than .500 in regular season play. Maloney's career .478 winning percentage remains the highest among Vancouver's 11 all-time coaches.

Gregg Boddy was truly versatile as he could play any forward position as well as defence.

Bill McCreary was practising "motivation" and a devotion to "total physical fitness." There was a distinct sense of optimism in the four-year-old franchise which stemmed from this new management team and a core-base of new impact players. No one was predicting overnight success, but the mood had progressed from "could *this* be the year?" to "this *could* be the year".

The first player to make an impact was Gary Smith. The big, brash netminder was an instant hit, even at his first press conference. Despite a reputation as being a "journeyman" goaltender, Smith addressed the media with guns blazing, proclaiming: "Yes, everything you've heard about me is absolutely true.... I *am* a tremendous goalie."

Meanwhile, 1st round pick Dennis Ververgaert was turning heads at the other end of the ice. The 20-year-old right winger from the OHA London Knights began slowly but caught fire as the season wore on, finishing with 26 goals and 31 assists for 57 points to finish second in team scoring behind Boudrias (16-59-75). New York Ranger GM Emile Francis noted at the time: "If Ververgaert had gotten off to a quicker start, he'd have been a front-runner in Calder Trophy (rookie-of-the-year) voting." As it was, he finished fifth in balloting, Denis Potvin of the Islanders being the winner.

Sophomore left winger Lever shrugged off the "second-year jinx" by connecting for 23 goals, up from 12 in his rookie year. Canuck management knew his future was solid as the name "Lever" was front and centre every time trade talks arose.

And, at first, it seemed "this *could* be the year." McCreary's charges got off to a flying start, going 5-4-1 in their first 10 games. But again, the club stumbled badly, winning but one of their next 19. The writing

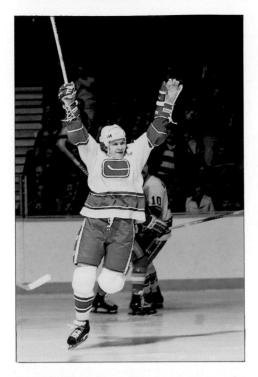

Canucks' "Iron Man", Don Lever, appeared in an incredible 437 consecutive games between Oct., '72 and Jan., '78. The durable left winger was Canucks' team captain in 1977-78 and 1978-79.

was on the wall and major changes were in the offing. On Jan. 14, 1974, McCreary was relieved of his duties and replaced behind the bench with longtime Western League Canuck Phil Maloney.

As a team, the Canucks finished up no closer than 17 points from a post-season playoff spot. But, individually, great strides were being made. Gary Smith put his pads where his mouth was and played in an unprecedented 65 games, recording 20 victories and three shutouts — all club records at the time. His candor and off-the-wall quirks (such as taking off all his equipment and putting it back on again between periods) made him a media favourite. And his on-ice performance made him a shoo-in for club MVP honours that season.

But, at last, the trade winds did blow. On Feb. 7, 1974, the Canucks engineered a deal which sent veteran Bobby Schmautz to the Boston Bruins for the big, young centre Chris Oddleifson, and winger Fred O'Donnell. And while O'Donnell never did report to the Canucks (he opted instead for the WHA), Oddleifson was to become a Vancouver fixture for the next eight seasons.

1974-75

During the '73-74 season, the club's original owner,

Rick Blight's most-feared weapon was his slapshot with which he terrorized goalies around the NHL.

Dennis Ververgaert began his career with a bang in 1973-74, connecting for 26 goals and 31 assists for 57 points. He remained a Canuck until 1978-79, scoring 304 career points in 409 games.

Tom Scallen, found himself in financial hot water. Scallen, a Minneapolis-based businessman, headed up a firm called Medicor (Medical Investment Corporation), a widely diversified company which encompassed medical equipment, office buildings, banks, and the highly successful Ice Follies.

During the first few years of the Canucks franchise, Scallen had borrowed money on several occasions to set his empire in order. All was well until one of his many money movements resulted in a charge of theft, an allegation for which he was subsequently convicted. In the summer of 1974, Scallen eventually sold the team for which he and his partners had paid $6 million four years earlier to local ownership for $9 million. The new purchaser was the Western Broadcasting Co., a communications conglomerate

The consummate utility man, Gerry O'Flaherty played 435 games for the Canucks between 1972 and 1977. "Flapper", as he was affectionately known, topped the 20-goal mark three times.

A scene from 1974-75, the divisional championship year, shows (L to R), Andre Boudrias, Leon Rochefort, John Grisdale, Bob Murray and Ken Lockett.

Remember these Canuck youngsters? From left to right, Ron Sedlbauer, Andy Spruce and Harold Snepsts.

owned by Frank A. Griffiths.

By the start of the 1974-75 season, with Griffiths, the new Board of Directors and GM/Coach Phil Maloney in full command, the team began to show definite signs of progress.

From the time they broke training camp in Victoria until the 28th of December, the Canucks ran roughshod over the rest of the NHL. Their October record was 5-3-2; November's was an incredible 10-3-2, while December saw them win seven, lose four and tie one. That tallies up to a 22-10-5 record after just 37 games, a heady .662 percentage. The club appeared destined for a truly phenomenal season. But suddenly, the wheels fell off.

It was New Year's Day, 1975. Canucks were hosting the defending Stanley Cup Champions, the Philadelphia Flyers. Flyer goalie Bernie Parent showed Canuck fans why his name would go on the Vezina Trophy that spring by snuffing out the locals 2-0. That game was a harbinger of worse things to come as Vancouver went on the road for six games, all of which were losses. Limping home with their tails between their legs, the Canucks lost two more at home before resuming their winning ways. So, in the midst of their

Frank Griffiths assumed ownership of the Canucks in 1974 and was promptly rewarded with a Divisional Championship in his first season.

finest NHL season in their first 20 years, the Canucks established a team record nine-game losing streak.

Over their final 34 games of the season, they went 16-13-5 to finish the year in first place in the Smythe Division (the first year of NHL realignment to the current divisional set-up) with 38 wins, 32 losses and 10 ties. Canucks were playoff-bound for the first time.

Unfortunately, under the new playoff format, the Canucks' post-season opponent turned out to be none other than the Montreal Canadiens. The Habs had proved a nemesis to the locals beyond any shadow of a doubt, forging a record of total domination consisting of 23 wins, three ties and *NO* losses. Vancouver opened at the Montreal Forum with a disappointing 6-2 loss but rebounded in Game Two with a 2-1 win, thanks to a winning tally by Garry Monahan. But it was downhill from there as the Canadiens won 4-1 and 4-0 here before eliminating the Canucks in the fifth game by a 5-4 score in overtime. The great Guy Lafleur registered the winning goal in three of the four Montreal victories. The season was sadly over for the locals but there was no denying great progress had been made.

Gary Smith gave a whole new meaning to the term "one-man show" as he played a staggering 72 games (more than any other NHL goaltender), posting a 32-24-9 record, a 3.09 goals-against average and a scintillating six shutouts. Smith's name was prominent when MVP time came around, but Flyers' Bobby Clarke copped the Hart Trophy as he led Philadelphia to a league-leading 51 wins while collecting 116 points himself.

Several other Canucks had career years in '74-75:

Whooping it up in the Canuck dressing room following the capture of the Smythe Division Championship in 1974-75. Vancouver finished with a 38-32-10 record, its best-ever showing. Note a very youthful Harold Snepsts in the middle of the back row in civvies.

Gary Monahan made four other NHL stops before becoming a Canuck in '74-75.

Boudrias led the club in scoring for his fourth and final time with 78 points.... Don Lever topped all teammates in goals with a career-high 38 (plus a personal best in points — 68).... Other Canucks who reached their highest career goals and points totals were: John Gould (34, 65); Paulin Bordeleau (17, 48) and Gerry O'Flaherty (25, 42).

And a big, raw rookie defenceman named Harold Snepsts played 27 games and had a goal and two assists. In his bio in the '74-75 Canucks yearbook, the last line prophetically states: "Vancouver fans would be wise to get used to his presence in a Canuck uniform. He'll be wearing one for years to come."

1975-76

What to do for an encore...? Though the Canucks came up against a brick wall in the playoffs, losing four games to one to the Canadiens, they had nonetheless shed the "weak sister" reputation they had established through their initial four NHL campaigns. Now the idea was to build on their '74-75 fortunes and keep the ball rolling.

In the amateur draft in June, '75, Canucks picked

One of the smoothest defencemen ever to play for the Canucks, Dennis Kearns patrolled the blueline for 10 seasons. In the three-year span between 1975 and 1978, he had seasons of 51 points, 60 and 47 while playing the full 80 games each campaign. All told, Kearns played 677 games for Vancouver and remains third in that department behind Stan Smyl and Harold Snepsts.

John Gould notched 34 goals in '74-75 and followed up with 32 the next campaign.

Harold Snepsts was a Canuck from 1974 to 1984 and then again from 1988 to 1990, playing a total of 781 games. He's the only player to have worn all four different jerseys the club has had in its history.

10th, selecting Rick Blight from the WHL Brandon Wheat Kings. The big (6'2", 190 lbs.) right winger rang up 60 goals and 52 assists in his final junior season and would shore up the right side of Vancouver's attack for several seasons.

The 1975-76 season got off on the right foot with a 3-2 road win at Minnesota. But for the next month, Canuck fans must have wondered if they'd suddenly

Paulin Bordeleau was as shifty and elusive as they came.

Dennis Ververgaert (#10) set a record for goals by a rookie with 26 in 1973-74, a mark which stood 'til 1988-89 when Trevor Linden scored 30.

gone back in time as Vancouver stumbled to a 3-8-3 record after 14 games. They did regain their composure, however, as they pulled their performance to the .500 mark by early January and maintained it the rest of the way, finishing with a 33-32-15 record. That put them a solid second in the final Smythe Division standings, just a single point behind Chicago.

For the second straight spring, Canucks drew the short straw when it came to a playoff opponent. This time it was the New York Islanders, a team that had skyrocketed to 101 points in the standings from a paltry 30 four seasons before. This time, the Canucks played a best-of-three series but again did not fare well, dropping the first game 5-3 at Long Island and the second 3-1 back home. This last game of '75-76 marked the end of an era for the Canucks as their perennial scoring leader Andre Boudrias played his final game in a Vancouver uniform. All told, he finished with 388 points in 458 games.

In retrospect, the '75-76 campaign had its bright

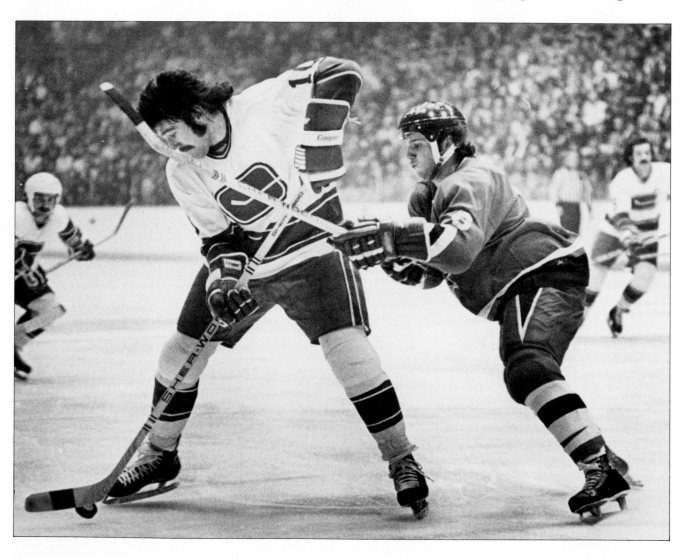

Towering Bob Dailey, seen here eluding the great Bobby Orr, was both imposing and talented. The 6'5", 220 lb. defenceman anchored the Canuck power-play for three-and-a-half seasons before being traded to Philadelphia in the deal that brought Jack McIlhargey to Vancouver.

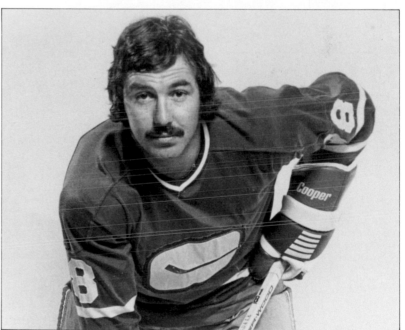

Never flashy but always steady, John Grisdale was a true "defensive" rearguard.

spots and its low points. True, the club did finish with its second-best record in history.... Dennis Ververgaert had his best NHL season with 37 goals and 34 assists to lead the club with 71 points.... Chris Oddleifson did the same with 16 goals and 62 points.... John Gould enjoyed a 32-goal season.... Rick Blight had a great freshman season with 25 goals and 56 points. But despite these highlights, they were bittersweet because the club had faltered after the successes of the year before. For Phil Maloney and his staff, it was back to the drawing board to figure out a new plan for 1976-77.

Defenceman Jack McIlhargey was a crowd favourite due to his hard-nosed, swashbuckling style of play.

A fine playmaking centre, Chris Oddleifson played eight seasons with the Canucks, captaining the club in 1976-77. He scored 265 points in 469 Vancouver games.

1976-77

Following its hasty exit from post-season play, Vancouver immediately set its sights on the '76-77 season. As mentioned the man who had worn jersey #7 so proudly for six seasons — Andre Boudrias — had retired. And via the deal in which they acquired goaltender Curt Ridley, Canucks did not have a first round pick in the 1976 Amateur Draft, having ceded their selection to the Atlanta Flames.

So, not only was their all-time scoring leader gone, but so was a chunk of the future. Canucks didn't choose until the 26th pick, selecting defenceman Bob Manno from St. Catharines of the OHA. They didn't make another major stir on the hockey scene until Aug. 23, 1976 when they parted with gregarious netminder Gary Smith who was dealt to the Minnesota

Free-spirited Ron Sedlbauer was Canucks' first 40-goal scorer. After shunting between the Canucks and the minors for several seasons, "Sudsy" struck for that total in 1978-79.

ABOVE RIGHT
Mike (Shaky) Walton led all Canucks in scoring in 1977-78 with 66 points. Fourteen of his 29 goals came on the power-play.

North Stars in exchange for Cesare Maniago.

Vancouver started the season off with a bang: sophomore right winger Rick Blight strafed Pittsburgh netminder Gord Laxton for four goals in the season-opening game and teammate Mike Walton earned four assists. Trouble was, the Penguins won the game 9-5, and the Canucks were off to another less-than-auspicious season debut. In fact, in their first 35 games, only nine were victories, while 23 losses and three ties were recorded. For many weeks, whispers rippled through Vancouver about changes being necessary. And three days before Christmas, conjecture became reality as Phil Maloney was replaced behind the bench by Orland Kurtenbach.

Kurtenbach had coached Canucks farm club in Seattle in 1974-75 and finished out of the playoffs. The following season, Vancouver CHL affiliation was transferred to Tulsa where Kurtenbach guided the Oilers to the League championship. In his NHL coaching debut, the big ex-Canuck captain led Vancouver to a 3-2 decision over Los Angeles, but then won only seven of the team's next 31 games. But late in the season, the team jelled and went on an unprecedented 10-game undefeated streak, winning five and tying five.

But, alas, the Canucks finished out of playoff contention with a 25-42-13 record.

Brad Gassoff was a hard-nosed left winger with a short fuse.

The most durable Canuck was Don Lever, the club's first-round draft pick in 1972, who played 437 straight games without missing one, and remains fourth in overall team scoring with 407 points in his eight-year career.

1977-78

On the final day of May, 1977, Canuck ownership announced a managerial change, replacing Maloney with veteran NHL executive Jake Milford. Milford had been in pro hockey for over four decades as a player, scout, coach, manager and administrator.

His first official function occurred two weeks later at the annual Amateur Draft in Montreal. Picking fourth over-all, the Canucks chose left winger Jere Gillis from Sherbrooke of the Quebec Junior League. They made another significant selection in the third round, taking goalie Glen Hanlon from the WHL Brandon Wheat Kings.

Again the Canucks broke quickly from the gate, forging a 3-1-2 record in the first six games. They were 10-12-7 by game #29 but then celebrated just 10 victories over the course of their final 52 contests to finish with a highly disappointing 20-43-17 record.

Mike Walton led the club in scoring with 29 goals (14 on the power-play, a club record), and 37 assists for 66 points.... Defenceman Dennis Kearns paced all teammates in assists with 43 (giving him 98 in two seasons).... Rookie Jere Gillis finished with 23 goals and 18 assists. But none of this was enough to deter Canuck management from replacing coach Kurtenbach with Harry Neale in May, 1978.

A new era lay directly ahead.

First-round draft pick Jere Gillis in his rookie year.

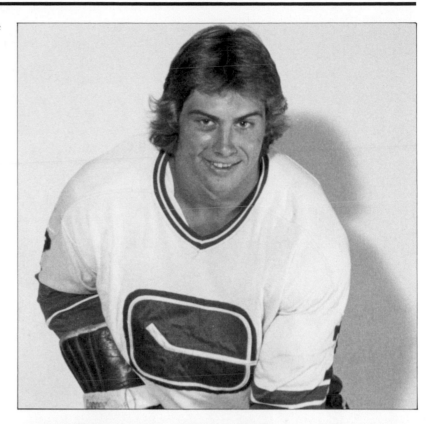

A new management duo arrived in 1977-78 with the tandem of Jake Milford (L) as General Manager and Orland Kurtenbach (R) as Coach.

A NEW REGIME

1978-79

The Canucks embarked on Season No. 9 in a striking new way. The traditional blue/green/white uniforms were discarded in favour of a bold and unique combination featuring gold, black and red. In addition, the old logo of hockey stick and rink was replaced by a dynamic, streaking stylized skate with the word "Canucks" forming the blade. Also prominent was a dramatic "V" on the front of the jersey to identify with "Vancouver". The entire new image was a rather startling departure from the norm and was greeted with great reaction throughout the hockey world.

As mentioned, GM Jake Milford had engaged Harry Neale as Head Coach. Neale had never played pro hockey but had a long and successful coaching career in the OHA with Hamilton, in U.S. college hockey at Ohio State and immediately prior to his posting with Vancouver had spent six seasons in the World Hockey Association with Minnesota and New England. During those six campaigns, Neale's teams never missed the playoffs. Neale's associate behind the bench was another WHA alumnus (and ex-Canuck defenceman) Dave Dunn.

In June, 1978, Milford and his scouting staff, headed by Jack MacDonald, selected three players in the Amateur Draft who were to have a great bearing on the future of the franchise. Centre Bill Derlago was selected in the first round (fourth overall) from Brandon of the WHL; Curt Fraser was picked second from Victoria, while a stocky right winger named Stan Smyl was chosen third from the Memorial Cup champion New Westminster Bruins. The latter selec-

Ron Sedlbauer added 16 assists to his 40 goals to lead the team in scoring in '78-79 with 56 points.

Stan Smyl and Rick Blight tuning up at 1978 training camp.

Glen Hanlon (L) receives some sage advice from another former Canuck netminder, Cesare Maniago, during an early video analysis.

Slick Swede Thomas Gradin was a rookie in '78-79 but went on to play eight seasons. He remains in second place in all-time team scoring with 550 points in 613 games. The fleet centre led Canucks in points twice, assists five times and goals once. And throughout his lengthy career in Vancouver, he was assessed only 280 minutes in penalties.

tion was met with raised eyebrows around the draft room as Smyl, though acknowledged as a real team leader, was nonetheless deemed by many scouts to be "too small and slow to make it in the NHL." Little did they know....

Not only were Milford & Co. very active in the draft, they went shopping in Europe that spring, too, specifically Sweden. The Scandinavian trio they landed consisted of centre Thomas Gradin and a pair of defencemen, Lars Lindgren and Lars Zetterstrom. Canuck fans attending training camp at Courtenay and pre-season games at the Coliseum that September truly needed a program to tell who was who on the new-look team.

In the season-opener, Neale iced a line which consisted of all rookies: Gradin at centre between Fraser on the left side and Smyl on the right. They liked each other's company right from the start as Gradin had two goals and an assist, Fraser a goal and an assist while Smyl chipped in with one assist. Vancouver hammered the Colorado Rockies, 8-2.

In 1978-79 Glen Hanlon played in 31 games with three shutouts and a goals-against average of 3.10. Hanlon remained a mainstay of the netminding corps until March, '82.

Harold Snepsts in his new '78-79 togs.

The '78-79 season featured radical new uniforms, three new Swedish players and new coach Harry Neale behind the bench. Neale remained in the organization for seven seasons as Coach and/or General Manager. He actually coached 407 Canuck games, the most of any Vancouver bench boss.

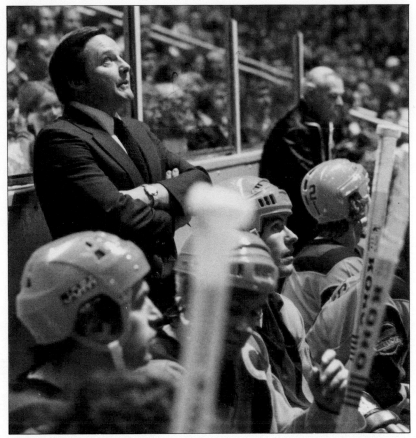

OPPOSITE PAGE:

Swedish defenceman Lars Lindgren was unspectacular but extremely steady through five seasons behind the Canuck blueline. A lasting trademark of Lars was his jersey, number 13; he was the only player ever to wear it.

The trio remained together all season except for a 17-game span when Smyl was sidelined with a bruised collarbone.

Here are some highlights from that season:

Nov. 1, '78... Glen Hanlon records his first NHL shutout, a 1-0 victory at Chicago.

Nov. 28, '78... Ron Sedlbauer tallies three goals in 6-3 win at St. Louis.

Dec. 29, '78... Vancouver trades Dennis Ververgaert to Philadelphia for defenceman Kevin McCarthy and forward Drew Callander.

Apr. 6, '79... Ron Sedlbauer becomes the first 40-goal scorer in club history as Vancouver concludes ninth NHL season with 2-2 tie against Minnesota. They finish second in the Smythe Division and prepare to meet their second-place counterparts in the Patrick Division, Philadelphia, in preliminary round of the playoffs.

Apr. 10, '79... Canucks surprise Flyers 3-2 in Philadelphia. Don Lever notches winning goal.

Apr. 12, '79... Canucks lose on home ice 6-4 as Flyers tally winner and empty-net goal in last minute of third period.

Apr. 14, '79... Canucks bow 7-2 to Philadelphia at Spectrum.

THE ROCKY ROAD TO THE FINALS

1979-80 to 1981-82

The 1979-80 season saw the amalgamation into the NHL of four former World Hockey Association teams: the Hartford Whalers, Quebec Nordiques, Winnipeg Jets and Edmonton Oilers, bringing the league to 21 teams. In the 1979 NHL Entry Draft, the Canucks selected Rick Vaive from the WHA Birmingham Bulls as their first-round pick.

Vancouver reeled off four straight wins in mid-November to bring their record to 9-5-5 in its first 19 games. The last victory in that streak was a 5-2 win over Montreal and it marked the first home-ice win over the Canadiens in Canuck history, thereby finally erasing a winless skein that had built to 0-15-6.

In December, General Manager Jake Milford made a couple of deals which saw Ron Sedlbauer sent to Chicago for Dave Logan and Harold Phillipoff, and another that landed Per-Olov Brasar from Minnesota for a future second-round draft pick.

The Canucks endured a tough December/January stretch during which they won just five of 26 games and which paved the way for a couple of true blockbuster trades engineered by Milford. On Feb. 7, 1980, Vancouver sent its all-time leading scorer Don Lever, along with utility winger Brad Smith, to the Atlanta Flames in exchange for left winger Darcy Rota and centre Ivan Boldirev. And just 11 days later, the Canuck GM again rocked the hockey world when he dealt Bill Derlago and Rick

The goaltending of Richard Brodeur helped propel the Canucks from mediocrity to the Stanley Cup Finals in 1982.

Thomas Gradin, a member of the 20-Year Dream Team, was often referred to as the "classiest" player ever to don a Vancouver uniform.

Vaive to Toronto for the legendary Dave (Tiger) Williams and right winger Jerry Butler.

Needless to say, the over-all "character" of the club changed dramatically. A mere four days after that swap, the fabled "Broad Street Bullies," the Philadelphia Flyers invaded the Coliseum. And though the Canucks lost the game, they suddenly served crystal-clear notice that they were no longer going to be pushed around as the feisty Williams and his mates engaged the rugged Flyers in altercations that generated 344 minutes in penalties. Williams himself started the ball rolling when he dropped the gloves with Flyer tough-guy Paul Holmgren in the first period, and continued his belligerent play in the second by fighting another rugged customer, Mel Bridgman. Even the goalies got into the act as Canucks' Glen Hanlon administered a sound thrashing to his Philadelphia counterpart Phil Myre.

Meanwhile, hard-working Stan Smyl was enjoying his finest season, scoring hat-tricks and setting club marks for consecutive-game point-scoring. He finished his second NHL season with 31 goals and 47 assists for 78 points, and his abrasive play earned him 204 penalty minutes. It marked the last time a player led his team in all four of those categories... and it made all his earlier detractors in scouting departments throughout the league eat their words.

Smyl's centre, Thomas Gradin, also turned in a fine season with 30 goals and 45 assists, while newcomer Boldirev finished the season with 27 points in as many Canuck games.

The Canucks finished third in their division, and through a complex playoff eligibility system, drew the Buffalo Sabres as a post-season opponent, a team that had finished 40 points ahead of them in the standings. In this best-of-five preliminary round, Canucks dropped a 2-1 squeaker to the Sabres and then were shut out 6-0 in Buffalo. They returned to Vancouver and defeated the Sabres 5-4 in an exciting, albeit unusual contest. In that game, Tiger Williams was involved in an incident at the Buffalo bench with several of the Sabre players. In the ensuing fracas, Buffalo coach Scotty Bowman was clipped by an errant stick "allegedly" belonging to Williams. The word "allegedly" is used because referee Bryan Lewis did not see what happened and didn't even call a penalty. But an NHL Supervisor of Officials, perched up in the press box some 200 feet away, claimed he saw Williams strike Bowman. Videotape of the incident revealed nothing but, nevertheless, NHL Executive Vice-President Brian O'Neill slapped the Vancouver forward with an

Rick Lanz remains Canucks' second all-time leading pointgetter among Vancouver defencemen with 227.

immediate suspension. Without their spiritual leader in the lineup, the Canucks lost their next game 3-1 and the series three games to one.

In June of '80, Canucks selected three players who would go on to have lengthy careers in Vancouver — defencemen Rick Lanz and Doug Lidster, and Swedish centre Patrik Sundstrom. And just prior to the start of the 1980-81 season, the wily Milford obtained three more players who would figure heavily in Canucks' future: he signed former Canuck original Bobby Schmautz as a free agent; he acquired veteran defenceman Colin Campbell in the Waiver Draft, and, in the one which produced the most impact, he swapped fifth-round amateur draft choices with the New York Islanders and got goalie Richard Brodeur in the process. Milford's puzzle was beginning to take shape.

In his first NHL game, Lanz carried the puck over the Detroit blue line, wound up for a slap shot (which he didn't take), faked Red Wing defenceman Rick Smith to the ice, and calmly deposited the puck behind goalie Jim Rutherford for the winning goal in the 5-3 contest. Six nights later in Philadelphia, Brodeur stopped 36 of 38 shots as he backstopped Vancouver to a 5-2 win in his Canuck debut.

The team, meanwhile, was off to its second-best start in history as it enjoyed a 17-9-9 record by Christmas. The debilitating January/February doldrums again took hold, however, and the team struggled through those two months at 5-14-7. They regrouped in March, though, and finished the season four games below .500 with 76 points, good for third place in the Smythe Division which, for the final season, was comprised of six teams. (St. Louis finished first, and Chicago second. Both teams vacated the Smythe the following season, moving to the Norris Division while Los Angeles left that group to join the Smythe.)

The club had developed a well-balanced scoring attack under Head Coach Harry Neale and his two new assistants, Roger Neilson and Ron Smith. In fact, for the first (and only) time in their history, the Canucks had eight 20-goal scorers. Leading the group was Tiger Williams who had a career-year with 35 goals to go along with his league-leading 343 penalty minutes. The other 20+ goal-men were: Schmautz (27); Boldirev (26); Smyl, Rota and Fraser (25 each); Brasar (22); and Gradin (21). Brodeur appeared in 52 games and had a 17-18-16 record.

For the second straight year, however, they drew the powerful Buffalo Sabres (99 points) as a playoff

Williams pairs off with big Willi Plett of the Flames. The rugged Canuck amassed 116 minutes in penalties in 17 playoff games.

opponent and were beaten by their expansion partners three straight. But the best was yet to come.

The Cinderella Year (1981-82)

As soon as the '80-81 season was over, Milford again went on a shopping spree, and his focus was on Europe. In May, he signed free agent Swedes Lars Molin and Anders Eldebrink... in the NHL Entry Draft he selected future Canuck Petri Skriko... and then in July he startled the hockey world by signing two Czech stars, Ivan Hlinka and Jiri Bubla. Other acquisitions who would have a major influence on future Canuck fortunes were first-round draft pick Garth Butcher from the Regina Pats and hard-nosed right winger Ron Delorme, picked up via the Waiver Draft from Colorado.

Here are some highlights from the '81-82 regular season:

Oct. 6, '81... Canucks begin 12th NHL season with a 4-2 win over Colorado and nine (9) Europeans in the lineup (5 Swedes, 3 Czechs, 1 Yugoslav).

Nov. 19, '81... Harold Snepsts plays in his 500th game as a Canuck.

Dec. 12, '81... Harold Snepsts becomes the first Canuck to surpass 1,000 minutes in penalties.

Feb. 11, '82... NHL history is made as both Thomas Gradin and Ivan Hlinka are awarded penalty shots in the same period against Detroit. Both Canuck players convert their opportunities against Red Wing goalie

Ron Delorme was a tower of strength for the Canucks against Chicago.

Gilles Gilbert. Final score, 4-4.

Mar. 9, '82... Milford engineers another major trade which sees netminder Glen Hanlon dealt to St. Louis for Jim Nill, Tony Currie, goaltender Rick Heinz and a fourth-round draft pick.

Mar. 20, '82... Thomas Gradin becomes first Canuck to record 80 points in a season.

Mar. 27, '82... Coach Harry Neale is handed a 10-game suspension for his involvement in an altercation with the crowd in Canucks' Mar. 20th game at Quebec. Defenceman Doug Halward is assessed a seven-game suspension in the same incident and Assistant Coach Roger Neilson takes over behind the bench.

Whatever happened in Quebec on March 20th caused a mystical change to come over the Canucks as a team. Maybe the incident drew the team closer together, or perhaps it brought the chemistry to just the right mix... whatever it was caused everything the club did to turn to gold.

Canucks went on to finish the season on a 6-0-3 tear for a final 30-33-17 record and set the stage for a magic carpet ride in the playoffs. Calgary Flames were

Brodeur savours series victory over the Los Angeles Kings.

their preliminary round opponent and, for the first time in club history, Canucks had home-ice advantage. It took Stan Smyl a mere eight seconds to score the first goal for Vancouver and the team was on its way to a 5-3 victory. The mood of the series was set just six seconds after Smyl's goal as Vancouver's Curt Fraser took on Calgary heavyweight Willi Plett in a fight, the first of many instances of hard feelings which would punctuate this short series. In fact, 224 minutes in penalties were called in only three games.

The Flames tightened things up in Game Two and a couple of unlikely marksmen — Ken Houston of Calgary and Marc Crawford of the Canucks — knotted the score 1-1 after three periods. Canuck goalie Richard Brodeur displayed the incredible netminding which would eventually carry the team to the Final, kicking out 33 of 34 Flames drives. At the 14:20 mark of the first overtime period, Lars Molin slid the puck over to Tiger Williams who was parked just to the right of Calgary goalie Pat Riggin. As he was being cross-checked to the ice by Flame defender Bob Murdoch, he backhanded an innocent looking shot through a maze of legs and into the net. Canucks won 2-1 and had a stranglehold on the series.

Back in the old Calgary Corral for Game Three, April 10, the Flames came out with guns blazing, outshooting Vancouver 15-5 in the opening period. But only Jim Peplinski could fool Brodeur on a Flame

Tiger Williams scores the winner in overtime in second game of series against Calgary. (If you look hard, you can see the puck sliding through the crease behind the upper part of Tiger's right leg and just below the #20 on Flame defenceman Bob Murdoch's right arm).

Roger Neilson...creator of "Towel Power" and pilot of Canucks' "Cinderella" flight to the Stanley Cup Finals in 1982.

There's little doubt as to which team won this 1982 home-ice playoff game.

power-play while Thomas Gradin did likewise for the Canucks on Riggin. The second period was scoreless but, again, the Flames peppered Brodeur with 15 shots while Vancouver managed just nine. Williams tallied at 8:17 of the third period with a goal which would stand as the winner, Gradin icing the contest with a marker at 17:59. Canucks had won their first-ever playoff series and they mobbed Brodeur when the game was over, for it was he who had provided the necessary netminding to douse the high-scoring Flames who had come into the series with three 30-goal scorers and five 20-goal men. Brodeur was merely brilliant, forging a 1.55 goals against average and stopping 103 of 108 shots in the series.

Next order of business... the Los Angeles Kings. The Kings, who had finished with 63 points in the Smythe Division standings, had pulled off the upset of the decade in their preliminary round series, beating Edmonton (which finished first, 48 points ahead of them) three games to two. Once again, Canucks had home-ice advantage.

Compared to the previous series, this was a relatively calm affair, especially in the first two games in Vancouver in which only minor penalties were assessed. Kings' Steve Bozek drew first blood but big Ivan Hlinka clicked twice in the second period on Canuck power-plays with an L.A. goal by Larry Murphy sandwiched between. Little buzz-saw Gary Lupul connected for Vancouver in the third to give

Centre Ivan Boldirev was at his best in the spring of '82, scoring eight goals and three assists in 17 games.

Canucks a 3-2 victory.

Canuck fans were beginning to believe this may be a team of destiny as they filled Pacific Coliseum to capacity for the first time in the playoffs for Game Two vs the Kings. Darcy Rota opened the scoring for Vancouver in the first period, then two-thirds of the fabled "Triple Crown Line" (Dave Taylor and Marcel Dionne [Charlie Simmer was the other]) made it 2-1 for Los Angeles before Stan Smyl tied the score. After a scoreless third, the two teams went to overtime with the pesky Bozek — always a thorn in the Canucks' side until he joined the team six years later — scoring the winner at 4:32 to send the throng of 16,413 home disgruntled.

The fireworks began in Game Three down at the Fabulous Forum in L.A. Gritty Jim Nill got into a scrap with Kings' Rick Chartraw which set the stage for a chippy game (76 penalty minutes). Canuck defenceman Colin Campbell, who hadn't scored a goal in 47 regular-season contests, got Vancouver on the board at the 18:09 mark of the first period. The Kings battled back in the second on two power-play markers before Gradin tied it 2-2 with just 45 seconds remaining. Dionne and Smyl traded third-period tallies to set up yet another overtime situation. Just 1:23 into the extra frame, Hlinka drew the puck back to the point to Campbell. He lobbed a shot towards the Kings' net which somehow managed to elude L.A. goalie Mario Lessard. Vancouver 4, Kings 3. And, oh yes, it was just another routine night for Brodeur; he kicked out 41 of 44 Kings shots!

The next night before another sellout crowd (16,005) at the Forum, Canucks scored first for the third time in a row, Ivan Boldirev getting the goal. Dionne replied on the power-play to knot the score 1-1 after one. Canucks broke it open in the second on three quick goals by the eight-minute mark to chase Lessard from the nets in favour of backup goalie Doug Keans. Kings scored twice more to trail by one going into the third. Boldirev scored his second of the night to lead off the third and Doug Smith tallied for L.A. But the Kings came no closer as Brodeur again slammed the door. The Canucks prevailed 5-4 despite being badly outshot, 37-16.

Vancouver could smell victory as they returned home for Game Five, April 21. But Bernie Nicholls silenced another capacity Coliseum crowd as he scored the game's first goal after just 90 seconds of play. The locals rallied, however, and led 2-1 after one on goals by Nill and defenceman Doug Halward. Rota tallied twice in the second period and Fraser in the third

Colin Campbell couldn't buy a goal in 47 regular season games but bagged two including the overtime winner Apr. 18, '82 in L.A.

while L.A. could muster but a single power-play marker. The Canucks had eliminated the Kings by a score of 5-2, taking the series four games to one. The delirious crowd stood and cheered their heroes that were fashioning a fairy tale and heading for the Stanley Cup Semi-Finals against the Chicago Blackhawks.

This time, there was no home-ice advantage and the Canucks had to open in the noisiest, most raucous arena in the NHL, Chicago Stadium. This was to be "*The* Classic Game" in the history of the Canucks franchise, and one of the most outstanding goal-tending duels of all time. Yet again, the Canucks struck first. Thomas Gradin scored at 8:02 on a pass from Curt Fraser. A scant two minutes later, Blackhawks' Terry Ruskowski tied it up and the score remained 1-1 through regulation time. Brodeur had cast aside 34 of 35 Chicago shots while his counterpart, Tony Esposito, had stopped 27 of 28 Vancouver drives.

Both teams continued their end-to-end play through the first overtime period in steamy Chicago stadium, the Hawks outshooting Vancouver nine to eight … but no goals. Eight minutes and 59 seconds into the second extra frame, Canucks were pressing in the

Stan Smyl (L) and Kevin McCarthy (R) pose with the Campbell Bowl. For McCarthy, it was a bittersweet moment, having suffered a fractured ankle two days before the playoffs began.

Chicago end. The Hawks tried sweeping the puck around the back of the net and up the right wing, but big Harold Snepsts intercepted it at the left point. He drifted a shot at the net which Esposito stopped. But the rebound came right to Jim Nill who snapped a high shot into the goal. The Canucks had just won the biggest game in their history.

More history was made in the following game two nights later. This was not to be Vancouver's night. Chicago's Glen Sharpley scored in the first period and Doug Feamster tallied in the second to give the Hawks a 2-0 lead. Stan Smyl got one back for the Canucks a minute into the third in a game that was getting chippier by the minute. Referee Bob Myers was handing out penalties left and right, but mostly to Vancouver. Slick Denis Savard scored to give the Hawks a 3-1 lead at 4:42 of the third and then all hell broke loose 15 seconds later when Canuck forward Gerry Minor got into a fight with Ruskowski. In the ensuing ruckus, Meyers handed out 74 minutes in penalties. Later that period, Meyers gave the Hawks

Doug Halward (L) and Stan Smyl (R) hoist the Campbell Bowl.

their ninth man-advantage of the game and Savard scored on the power-play at 16:23 to give Chicago a commanding 4-1 lead.

After the goal was scored, Canuck coach Roger Neilson immediately reached for a spare hockey stick, grabbed a white towel off the clothesline behind the bench and hoisted towel and stick high over his head in a gesture of surrender to referee Meyers. Several players on the bench reached for towels and copied their coach and Meyers responded by ... you guessed it ... handing out more penalties. Hawks went on to win the game 4-1 and Neilson was slapped with a heavy fine by the NHL.

When the Canucks returned home to resume their

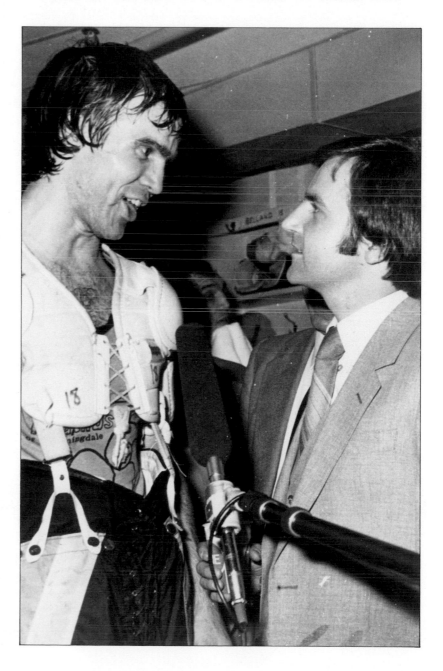

Darcy Rota does post-game victory interview with BCTV sportscaster Ron Manz.

series against the Hawks three days later, they were greeted by 16,413 fans who, besides giving them a standing ovation, were waving white towels. Neilson had unwittingly created a rallying ritual which would characterize all home games the rest of the way. In a much more sedate game, the Canucks and "Towel Power" beat the Hawks at the Coliseum 4-3 in Game Three. Stan Smyl scored the winning goal.

Game Four was another penalty-filled contest in which the Canucks roared to a 3-0 lead and then survived a late Chicago surge (thanks to Brodeur, who

Jim Nill, author of the biggest goal in Canuck's history.

for the eighth time since the playoffs began, was named either the first or second star of the game), winning 5-3. It was only the fourth game of the series, but it was to be the last Canuck fans saw of the Blackhawks.

Just as they had in the preceding series against Los Angeles, Canucks again sensed they had the opposition on the ropes. And despite the fact they were returning to hostile Chicago Stadium, scene of the last of their only playoff defeats to date, they exuded confidence. The visitors quickly negated the roaring crowd by jumping to a 2-0 lead after only three minutes and 48 seconds, thanks to Jim Nill and Stan Smyl. Tom Lysiak got one back for the Hawks but Lars Molin restored the two-goal lead with the eventual game-winner before the first period was over. And what a first period it was!

A fierce donnybrook broke out at the 7:43 mark and flared up again just before the period ended. Three

Kevin McCarthy preceded Stan Smyl as Canucks captain. McCarthy, a fine rushing defenceman, scored 143 points in his first three seasons as a Canuck. His darkest hour came at the end of the '81-82 season when he fractured his ankle in practice, a mishap which kept him out of the team's Cinderella ride through to the '82 Stanley Cup Finals.

Neil Belland came from relative obscurity to lead all Canuck defencemen in scoring in the 1982 playoffs.

different fights punctuated the last episode, the highlight being a unanimous decision by Ron Delorme over Chicago's Grant Mulvey. When the smoke had cleared, the referee had assessed a staggering 164 minutes in penalties to both clubs. And though the Hawks outshot Vancouver 38-28 in the game, it was the Canucks who outscored Chicago 3-1 the rest of the way to win convincingly 6-2. Thus the Hawks were eliminated four games to one and the Cinderella Canucks had captured their first Clarence Campbell Bowl, emblematic of Campbell Conference supremacy.

NHL Vice President Brian O'Neill was on hand to present the prestigious trophy to interim team captain Smyl and his injured teammate and captain Kevin McCarthy, and to congratulate all the Canucks, including Coach Neilson upon whom he'd levied that fine just eight days prior in the infamous "towel-raising" incident.

The champagne flowed freely in the Canucks dressing room while the stereo pumped out the pop tune that the team had adopted as its victory song that spring, "Freeze Frame" by the J. Geils Band. None of the Canucks had ever had anything like this to celebrate in the NHL before, and many had been in the League a long time. They savored the moment like a fine wine ... but not for long.

Fact was, they had a date with the defending Stanley Cup champion New York Islanders just two days later. So without the luxury of a trip home to celebrate with loved ones and pick up a change of clothes, the merry Canuck band headed straight to Long Island.

The New York newspapers had little but disdain for the "upstarts from the West Coast," but that didn't deter the Canucks who stormed out in Game One of the Stanley Cup final and grabbed an early 1-0 lead on a goal by Thomas Gradin. Veteran Clark Gillies, on the power-play, and sniper Mike Bossy tallied for the Islanders before Gradin got his second of the period on a Canuck man-advantage. And before the period's end, Isles went up 3-2 on another power-play marker by All-Star defenceman Denis Potvin.

When Potvin notched another goal with just 3:15 gone in the second period, fans in Nassau Coliseum nodded knowingly, sensing a rout by their team. But the gritty, never-say-die Canucks clawed their way even again on goals by Stan Smyl and Ivan Boldirev. And there was an audible "gulp" when Jim Nill put Vancouver ahead 5-4 with just seven minutes left in the third period. But then the elusive Bossy connected for his second of the night and the game headed into overtime.

During the intermission between the third period and overtime, the press box in Nassau Coliseum was abuzz about the Vancouverites. Comments like "this wasn't in the script" and "who *are* these guys?" characterized conversations. Both clubs played cautiously in the overtime frame taking just six shots apiece. And as the final minute wound down, it looked as if the Canucks would again extend a playoff opponent into a second extra period. But as the last seconds ticked away, Bossy pounced on a loose puck in the Canuck zone and drilled a high shot past a helpless Richard Brodeur.

Harold Snepsts and Richard Brodeur combine to thwart Mike Bossy.

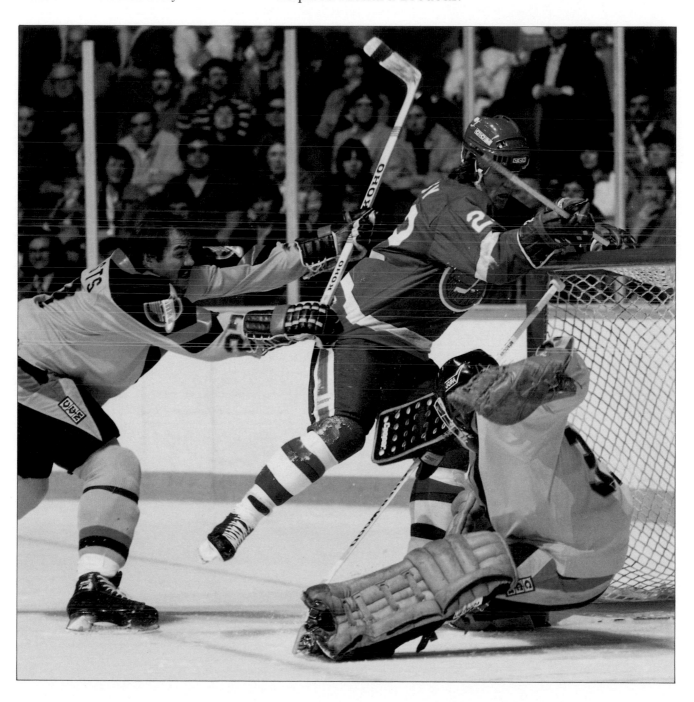

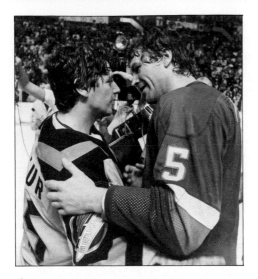

Vancouver's '82 playoff MVP Richard Brodeur receives congratulations from Islanders' Denis Potvin.

Invading Billy Smith's goal-crease was no day at the beach, as Darcy Rota will attest.

After the Canucks had played so well, it was a crushing defeat and the players and coaches took little solace from the consensus drawn by the media after the game that: "only a Mike Bossy could have scored that goal." They simply had to put it behind them and look ahead to Game Two.

The second contest didn't start well for the Canucks as the Islanders opened the scoring while short-handed. But Canucks stormed back in the second with two power-play goals by Gradin and Boldirev, plus an even-strength tally by Lars Lindgren. Bossy scored for the Isles who then trailed 3-2 going into the final period. That frame belonged to New York as four different Islanders scored while Gerry Minor was the only Canuck to fool netminder Billy Smith. Final score, 6-4 Islanders.

Neilson's band was clearly disappointed, having surrendered leads going into the third period in both games at Long Island. But now they were heading home to the friendly confines of Pacific Coliseum where they'd only played two of their last seven games.

The team was totally unprepared for the welcoming committee at Vancouver Airport. As Canucks' plane touched down, a group of airport fire trucks raced alongside down the runway with towels hoisted on hockey sticks! And after clearing customs, the team was confronted by a crowd of well-wishers that numbered between 25 and 30 thousand. Once the players reached the team bus, it took the vehicle over an hour to cover the two miles from the airport to the Arthur Lang Bridge!

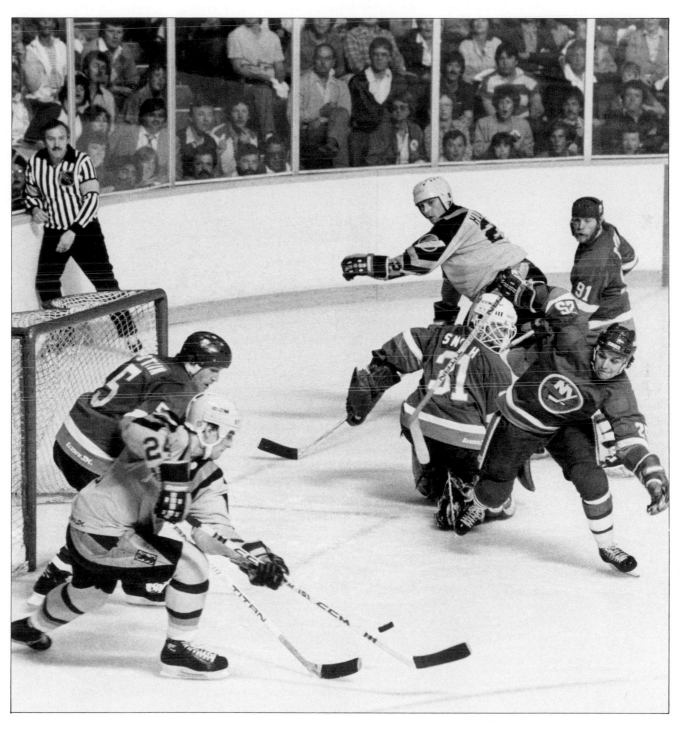

Curt Fraser (#24) battles Denis Potvin (#5) for loose puck as Islander goalie Billy Smith gets caught out of position.

The scene which greeted the team at the Coliseum that Thursday, May 13, 1982 was one of total bedlam. While ticket scalpers had a field day outside the building, the 16,413 fans inside were raising the roof and buying up every last unit from the white towel concession. The game itself was frustration personified. The team that had no trouble scoring goals — 20 in its last four games — suddenly was gripping its sticks so tightly, the sawdust was almost coming out of them. The tic-tac-toe passes didn't click and the shots were rushed and off target. In its overwhelming desire to reward its long-suffering fans, the club had a bad case of the jitters. They simply couldn't put a puck past Billy Smith, who stopped all 23 Canuck shots on goal. Meanwhile, at the other end of the rink, Clark Gillies and Mike Bossy scored second-period goals, and Bob Nystrom iced it with an empty-netter in the third.

Down three games to none, the Canucks clearly had their backs against the wall. The team had three days to contemplate the fact that no team had overcome that deficit in a final series since Toronto came back to win four straight after being down three games to Detroit in 1942.

Canucks were again behind the eight ball in Game Four as Butch Goring opened the scoring for the Islanders halfway through the first period. Canuck fans finally had something to cheer about seven minutes later as Stan Smyl scored through sheer determination while being cross-checked to the ice. But that was to be all the Canucks could muster as Billy Smith and his teammates slammed the door on Vancouver. The irrepressible Mike Bossy scored a pair of power-play goals three minutes apart in the second period and that's how it stayed ... 3-1 for the Islanders. For Team Cinderella, midnight had arrived.

As the two teams shook hands at centre ice and Islander captain Bryan Trottier took the ceremonial skate around the ice with the Stanley Cup over his head, Canuck fans stood and cheered their underdog heroes long and loud. They even cheered when it was announced that Bossy, who had scored 17 goals in 19 playoff games (seven of them against the Canucks), had won the Conn Smythe Trophy as playoff MVP. The locals had nothing to be ashamed of; they'd come farther than anyone could have imagined in their wildest dreams and they could hold their heads high with pride.

The next day (Monday, May 17) nearly 100,000 Vancouverites goofed off work to attend a parade arranged by civic officials. The parade route ran from

This was the scene at English Bay the day most of Vancouver turned out to pay tribute to their Stanley Cup finalist Canucks.

The happy gang visited Mayor Harcourt's office at City Hall and received citations of civic recognition.

the north foot of Burrard Street the full length of that thoroughfare and finished up at Sunset Beach where the largest portion of the crowd had gathered to hear speeches and be part of the final player introductions. Then-Mayor Mike Harcourt later hosted a reception for all players and management at City Hall where everyone signed the City Register and received a leather-bound citation of civic recognition from Harcourt. Then it was back to the Pacific National Exhibition for a reception by PNE President Erwin Swangard. All in all, it was an incredible display of support, especially in view of the fact that the team had lost the series. One can only imagine what the scene would have been like had the Canucks won the Cup!

As a final gesture of gratitude, the Griffiths family rewarded each player and member of team management with a miniature replica of the Clarence Campbell Bowl, a fitting and highly-appreciated tribute to a team which came of age virtually overnight.

This was the towel-waving mob that greeted the Islanders before the third game of the 1982 Stanley Cup Finals in Vancouver.

THE MID-EIGHTIES

1982-83 to 1986-87

Just 16 days after the final playoff game in 1982, the Canucks solidified their management team by promoting Jake Milford to the position of Senior Vice-President, elevating Harry Neale to General Manager, and making Roger Neilson the Head Coach. On June 9, 1982, Vancouver selected Michel Petit 11th overall in the NHL Entry Draft. The big French Canadian defenceman would go on to play 226 games for the Canucks over the next four-plus seasons.

After such an incredible spring, the Canucks and their fans were champing at the bit to get started again for the '82-83 season. Many observers felt that the club had finally turned that elusive corner and the winning formula had been found. But, unfortunately, more frustration lay ahead.

1982-83

Oct. 5, '82...Canucks meet the Islanders in their home-opener and win 2-1. Prior to the game, banners are raised signifying the 1982 Campbell Conference Championship, a salute to towel-power, plus a long-overdue banner to commemorate their Smythe Division title of 1974-75.

Nov. 14, '82...Thomas Gradin becomes the fifth and fastest Canuck to reach 300 points as he achieves the feat in his 330th game, a 6-5 loss at Winnipeg.

Jan. 6, '83...Darcy Rota scores his second hat-trick as a Canuck in a 7-4 win in Hartford. The same day, Curt Fraser is traded to Chicago for Tony Tanti.

Jan. 15, '83...Ivan Boldirev is traded to

Darcy Rota celebrates an '82-83 goal against the Jets. Rota duplicated this kind of scene 41 other times that season to finish with a record 42 goals and 39 assists for 81 points.

Arthur Griffiths was named Assistant to the Chairman of the Canucks in 1982. His first major task was to hammer out a new lease agreement with the PNE for the Pacific Coliseum.

Detroit for Mark Kirton.

Feb. 4, '83...Anders Eldebrink is traded to Quebec for goaltender John Garrett.

Mar 27, '83...Darcy Rota sets a club record with his 42nd goal of the season during an 8-4 win over Los Angeles.

April 3, '83...Vancouver concludes its 13th season with three 80+ point players — Stan Smyl, 88 (a club record), Thomas Gradin, 86, and Darcy Rota, 81.

1983-84

June 8, '83...Canucks select Cam Neely ninth overall in NHL Entry Draft.

Oct. 7, '83...Canucks win the highest-scoring game in team history, defeating Minnesota 10-9. Patrik Sundstrom broke a 9-9 tie, scoring the winner at 15:04 of the third period. Six of the Canuck goals came on the power-play.

Oct. 20, '83...Lars Lindgren, who had played 335 games for the Canucks over five seasons, is dealt to Minnesota for a future draft choice.

Nov. 16, '83...In a game at Los Angeles, Tony Tanti scores a point that gives him 19 goals and 15 assists for 34 points in only his 19th game of the season, the fastest start ever by a Canuck.

Jan. 4, '84...Thomas Gradin scores his 408th point to move past Don Lever into first place in all-time Canuck scoring.

Just prior to their 1982-83 home-opener, Vancouver raised banners signifying their 1975 Smythe Division Championship plus their '82 Campbell Conference and Smythe titles.

Jan. 19, '84...Roger Neilson is replaced as Head Coach by GM Harry Neale. Neilson's record behind the Canuck bench was 51-61-21 in 133 regular season games and 12-9 in playoffs.

Jan. 26, '84...Former captain Kevin McCarthy is traded to Pittsburgh for a future draft choice.

Jan. 31, '84...Darcy Rota represents Canucks at NHL All Star game in New Jersey.

Feb. 3, '84...1982 playoff hero Jim Nill is sent to Boston for Peter McNab.

Feb. 29, '84...Patrik Sundstrom explodes for a goal and six assists during a 9-5 rout of Pittsburgh, establishing club records for assists and points in a single game.

Mar. 30, '84...Tony Tanti scores his 45th goal of the season, a new team record. Canucks end 14th season with a record 306 goals scored, and a 32-39-9 record.

The hottest-scoring line of the mid-eighties was (L to R) Tony Tanti at right wing, Patrik Sundstrom at centre, with Petri Skriko on left wing.

Big Jim Sandlak was Canucks' first-round draft pick in 1985 and made the NHL's All-Rookie team at right wing.

One of the finest playmakers ever to wear a Canuck jersey was Patrick Sundstrom who set a club record in 1983-84 by scoring 91 points. Included in that total was a single game record seven points (a goal and six assists) vs Pittsburgh, Feb. 29, '84.

OPPOSITE PAGE:

"King" Richard Brodeur blocks one of thousands of shots he faced during 377 appearances in goal over eight Canuck seasons. Brodeur was Vancouver's all-time leader in goal with 126 victories.

Apr. 7, '84...Richard Brodeur shuts out Calgary 7-0 to register Canucks' first blanking of an opponent in playoff action. Defenceman Doug Halward scores a hat-trick.

1984-85

May 18, '84...Canucks hire 33-year-old Bill LaForge as the eighth coach in team history.

June 9, '84...Canucks, drafting 10th, select J.J. Daigneault as first pick in NHL Draft.

June 21, '84...Harold Snepsts is traded to Minnesota for left winger Al MacAdam.

Aug. 8, '84...Tiger Williams is traded to Detroit for left winger Rob McClanahan.

Stan Smyl connects against the Nordiques, one of a franchise-leading 260 goals "The Steamer" scored up 'til the end of the '89-90 season.

OPPOSITE PAGE:

Tony Tanti, Canucks' All-Star rep in 1985-86, was Vancouver's most prolific scorer of the eighties. In the five seasons between 1983 and 1988, Tanti tallied 204 goals, an average of just over 40 per year.

81

A solid rearguard and classic bodychecker was Jiri Bubla who came from Czechoslovakia in 1981-82 with Ivan Hlinka, and went on to play 256 games for Vancouver.

Jack Gordon joined the Canucks in 1980 and became the club's GM in 1985. His entire career was spent in hockey dating back to his playing days in the New York Ranger organization in the fifties.

Marc Crawford was an honest, two-way winger who played in 176 Canuck games.

Sept. 25, '84...Jake Milford is bestowed hockey's highest honour — election to the Hockey Hall of Fame.

Nov. 21, '84...Bill LaForge is replaced by Harry Neale behind the Canuck bench after just 20 games as coach, the shortest tenure of any coach in team history. LaForge's record was 4-14-2.

Feb. 12, '85...Thomas Gradin is Canucks' representative in the NHL All Star Game played in the Calgary Saddledome.

Feb. 27, '85...Stan Smyl scores his 187th goal to pass Don Lever as Canucks' all-time leading goal-scorer.

Mar. 8, '85...Thomas Gradin scores the 500th point

Tiger Williams the "All Star" in the 1981 NHL classic.

of his NHL career, becoming the first Canuck to reach that milestone.

1985-86

June 4, '85...Jack Gordon is named Director of Hockey Operations and General Manager, replacing Harry Neale. He becomes Canucks' sixth GM.

Petri Skriko more than doubled his point totals in 1985-86, notching 78 compared to just 35 in his rookie year.

Stan Smyl was always referred to as the "heart and soul" of the Canucks. The photo at left shows Smyl as the captain of the Memorial Cup champion New Westminster Bruins in 1977. In the main picture, he mixes it up a few seasons later with the Montreal Canadiens.

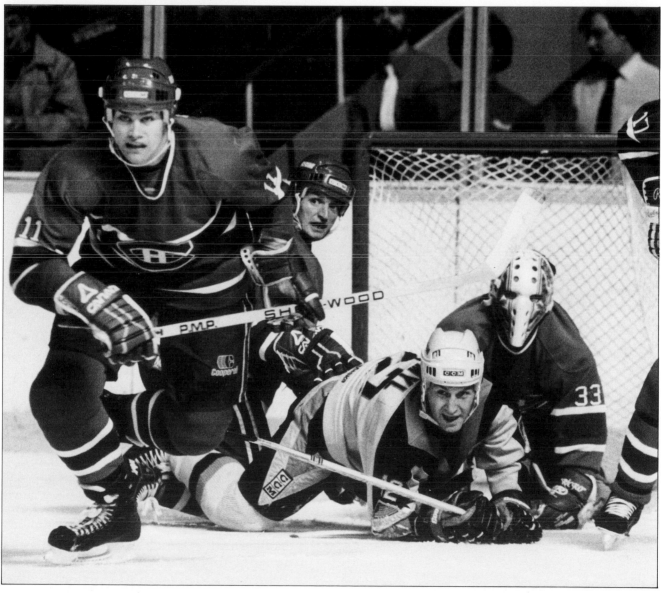

A cornerstone of the defence corps through the late eighties, Doug Lidster set a new standard for blueliners in 1986-87 by scoring 63 points.

June 15, '85...Jim Sandlak is Canucks' first pick (fourth overall) in NHL Entry Draft.

June 20, '85...Tom Watt is signed as Head Coach, the ninth in team history.

Nov. 11, '85...Richard Brodeur blanks Detroit 5-0, the same score by which he shut out the Wings just 19 days earlier.

Nov. 22, '85...Stan Smyl becomes first Canuck to score 200 career goals.

Feb. 4, '86...Tony Tanti, Canucks' All Star rep, opens the scoring for Campbell Conference All Stars who lose 4-3 to Prince of Wales team in Hartford.

Though never a prolific scorer, little Gary Lupul was always a crowd favourite due to his buzz-saw, never-quit style of play.

Feb. 26, '86...Richard Brodeur becomes the first Canuck netminder to appear in 300 games.

Apr. 6, '86...Canucks wind up their 16th season. Petri Skriko is Vancouver's leading scorer with 38-40-78. Thomas Gradin plays his final regular season game as a Canuck finishing as the team's career leader in assists (353) and points (550). These marks were later erased by Stan Smyl.

1986-87

June 6, '86...Canucks trade Cam Neely and their first pick in the 1987 draft to Boston for Barry Pederson. They also deal J.J. Daigneault and two draft picks to Philadelphia for Rich Sutter, Dave Richter and a draft choice.

Oct. 11, '86...Canucks open season #17 with a 4-3 win over St. Louis. Petri Skriko tallies the winner while the Canucks are short-handed.

Nov. 26, '86...Petri Skriko scores his third hat-trick in just eight days as Canucks beat L.A. 5-3. Skriko's scoring tear earned him NHL Player-of-the-Week honours (Nov. 17-23) as he scored an incredible 12

Pat Quinn comes full circle, from Canuck player in 1970, to President and General Manager in 1987. The ever-present stogie is a Quinn trademark throughout the NHL.

OPPOSITE PAGE:

Hard-nosed defenceman Garth Butcher had a lot of dealings with NHL referees as he led Canucks in penalty minutes for five straight seasons (1985 through 1989).

goals and two assists in a span of only five games.

Dec. 2, '86...Rick Lanz is traded to Toronto for Jim Benning and Dan Hodgson.

Dec. 14, '86...Stan Smyl scores the sixth hat-trick of his career, leading Canucks to a 7-3 win over Chicago. His third goal was also the 551st point of his career, moving him past Thomas Gradin as the club's all-time scoring leader.

Jan. 9, '87...Pat Quinn, Head Coach of the Los Angeles Kings, accepts post of President and GM of Canucks. His actions draw a suspension and heavy fines from League President John Ziegler. (The original fine to the Canucks in the amount of $310,000 was subsequently reduced to $10,000 by the U.S. Supreme Court).

Mar. 6, '87...Petri Skriko scores his fourth hat-trick of the season, a club record, to pace Canucks to a 4-1 win over Montreal.

Apr. 5, '87...Canucks finish their 17th season by winning their seventh home game in a row. Lidster established a new mark for points in a season by a defenceman with 63.... Tony Tanti finishes with 41 goals to become first Canuck ever to record back-to-back 40-goal campaigns.

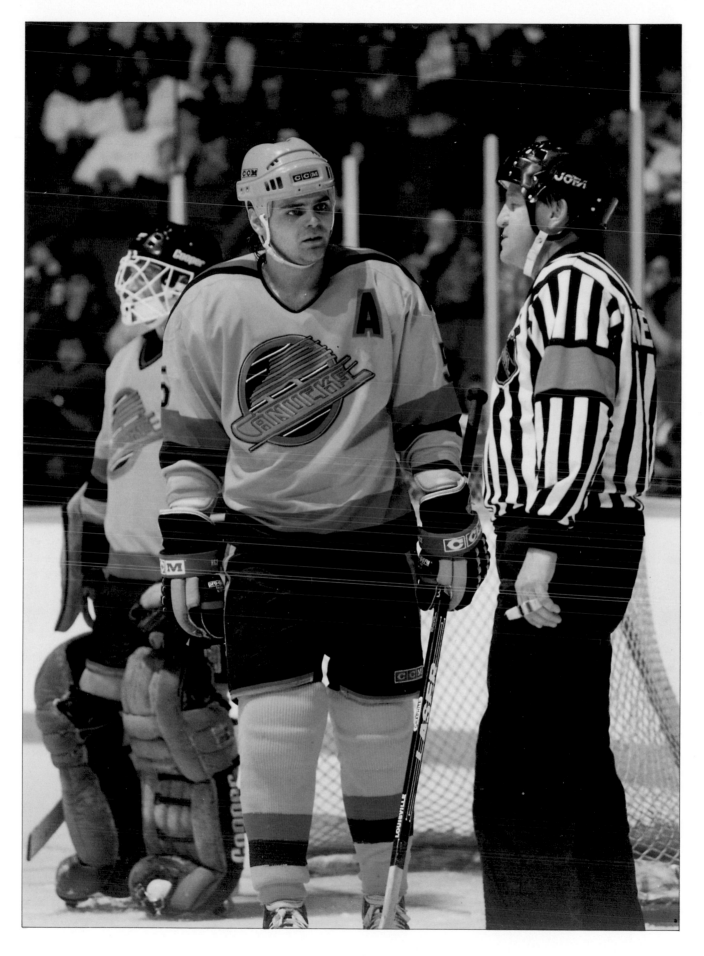

THE MODERN ERA

During the spring of '87, the Canucks set about fighting the NHL ruling which suspended Pat Quinn and fined the hockey club for the latter's signing with Vancouver while still under contract with the Kings. The Canucks contended that Quinn had acted in an honourable fashion and that the fine ($310,000) and suspension were "beyond the power of the League President and clearly excessive."

In the subsequent months, the legal action paid off for the Canucks. Quinn was permitted to assume his role as team President on May 1, 1987, and in early November, the B.C. Supreme Court ruled that Ziegler had indeed overstepped his authority in the case, and the fine was reduced to $10,000.

Meanwhile, Quinn busily attacked his new duties of building a new management team. On June 2, 1987, he hired former player and Harvard Law School grad Brian Burke as Vice President and Director of Hockey Operations. And just 20 days later, Bob McCammon was named the team's Head Coach for 1987-88. This trio (along with assistant coach Jack McIlhargey) was steeped in Philadelphia Flyers tradition. Quinn and McCammon had each coached the Flyers in the early '80s (the latter having been GM, too, in 1983-84); Burke had been a player with their minor league affiliate in Maine; and McIlhargey had played defence for Philadelphia from 1974 to 1977 and again from 1979 to 1981. This Philadelphia connection was highlighted on the cover of the 1987-88 Canuck Yearbook as it featured a photo of Quinn, Burke and McCammon, suitcases in

Greg Adams rebounded from a mediocre '88-89 to lead the Canucks with 30 goals last season.

91

Canucks' new management team which arrived on the scene for the '87-88 season had a distinct Philadelphia Flyer upbringing. Pat Quinn (L) and Bob McCammon (R) both coached and managed the Flyers while Brian Burke (C) was a player in their farm system.

hand, in front of a road-sign declaring Vancouver ahead and Philly behind.

Now in the GM's chair, Quinn began rebuilding the Canuck roster. On Aug. 31, '87, he traded goalie Wendell Young and a draft choice to the Flyers for Daryl Stanley and Darren Jensen. And two weeks later, he orchestrated his first blockbuster deal, sending Patrik Sundstrom to New Jersey for centre Greg Adams and netminder Kirk McLean, plus an exchange of assorted draft picks.

Adams wasted no time endearing himself to Canuck fans as he fired in four goals in Canucks' 1987-88 home-opener, an 8-2 drubbing of the St. Louis Blues. The team's on-ice performance that season was a forgettable 25-46-9 for 59 points and a fifth-place finish in the Smythe Division. But away from the rink, Quinn kept up his wheeling and dealing in an effort to build a winner.

In a flurry of deals prior to the March, 1988 trading deadline, Quinn sent Willie Huber to Philadelphia for Paul Lawless and a draft pick ... traded Craig Coxe to Calgary for Brian Bradley, Kevan Guy and Peter Bakovic ... and dealt Richard Brodeur to Hartford for goalie Steve Weeks. With a disappointing '87-88 season behind them, it was time for the Canucks to take dead aim at season #19.

Bob McCammon can be very vocal behind the Canucks bench.

First order of business was the NHL Entry Draft, on June 11, 1988. Selecting second behind Minnesota, Canucks picked right winger Trevor Linden from the WHL Medicine Hat Tigers, a player who was to be a cornerstone of the new-era Canucks. Then, just prior to training camp in the Vancouver Island town of Parksville, Quinn made a couple more heady deals. First, he acquired all-star defenceman Paul Reinhart and veteran winger Steve Bozek from Calgary in exchange for a third-round '89 draft choice; then he traded Dave Richter to St. Louis for defenceman Robert Nordmark and Blues 1990 second-round draft pick. The same day, Quinn delighted longtime Canuck fans by re-acquiring free agent defenceman Harold Snepsts. In the space of one short year, Quinn had overhauled the Canucks to the tune of an amazing 18 new faces! By the time the new season rolled around, Canuck fans really did need a program to figure out the vastly-changed roster.

For the first two weeks of the season, the team won just one of its first seven games, and it looked like a case of "here we go again!" But the Canucks gradually got it together and played close to .500 hockey for the remainder of the schedule. Trevor Linden quickly demonstrated why he was a No. 1 draft pick by scoring

Garth Butcher is as proficient with his verbal jabs as he is on defence and often goads opponents into foolish penalties.

Assistant coach Jack McIlhargey is still a "holler guy" as a coach, just as he was as a player.

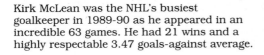

Kirk McLean was the NHL's busiest goalkeeper in 1989-90 as he appeared in an incredible 63 games. He had 21 wins and a highly respectable 3.47 goals-against average.

his first hat-trick vs Minnesota, Nov. 17, and then duplicating the feat just five days later against Buffalo. Linden went on to enjoy a banner rookie year, scoring a club record 30 goals and adding 29 assists for 59 points. (And following a fine playoff performance, he was voted The Hockey News NHL Rookie-of-the-Year, as selected by fan balloting.)

Meanwhile, at the other end of the rink, Kirk McLean was blossoming into a bonafide NHL netminder. The big Toronto native appeared in 42 regular-season contests and had a record of 20 wins, three ties and 17 losses, a sparkling 3.08 goals-against average and four shutouts.

Defenceman Paul Reinhart, who was something of an uncertainty when he came to the Canucks from the Flames due to a wonky back, silenced the skeptics while quarterbacking the team's power-play. He tallied seven goals and 50 assists in 64 games, 39 of his points coming while the Canucks enjoyed the man-advantage.

As far as the team was concerned, February 1989

Paul Reinhart once again showed his creativity by finishing second in Canuck scoring in '89-90 with 17 goals and 40 assists for 57 points. Reinhart was again the quarterback of the Vancouver power-play with nine of his goals coming while the Canucks enjoyed the man advantage.

appeared to be a turning point. Following a 5-4 victory at Buffalo, Feb. 10, the club went on a tear, winning their next six games to establish a franchise-record seven-game winning streak. They finished the season with 33 wins (the first time in 13 seasons they'd reached that total), 39 losses and eight ties. They also gave up just 253 goals, the lowest in team history, and 67 fewer than the season before. And who did they draw as their Stanley Cup Quarter-Final Series opponent? Merely the Calgary Flames, who'd finished first over-all in the NHL with 54 victories and 117 points in the standings!

This series obviously didn't promise to be a barn-burner. "Underdog Smurfs" proclaimed The Province pre-series headline... "Canucks lack the firepower the Flames enjoy" trumpeted The Vancouver Sun. Ignoring these pronouncements, the Canucks invaded the Saddledome on April 5, 1989, and spanked the Flames 4-3 on an overtime goal by ex-Calgary defenceman Reinhart. McLean was spectacular in goal, stopping 43 of 46 shots. Suddenly, the headlines changed to such

phrases as: "Flames Aren't Crisp" ... "Canucks No Joke" ... and "Doubt creeps into Flames game."

The next two games, however, were a different story. The Flames rebounded with a 5-2 home-ice victory in Game Two and drubbed the locals 4-0 back at the Pacific Coliseum in the third contest. Things were looking grim for McCammon's troops.

But the gritty Canucks were determined not to go down without a fight, and with rookie Trevor Linden picking his mates up by the bootstraps with a goal and three assists, Canucks snapped back to win game #4, 5-3, to even the series at two games apiece.

The Jekyll & Hyde Flames returned home with a vengeance and totally shut down the Canuck attack in Game Five, blanking Vancouver 4-0 for the second time in the series while outshooting the Canucks 40-18. Calgary goalie Mike Vernon was invincible in recording his second series shutout.

Down three games to two, the Canucks had their backs to the wall as they returned to the friendly confines of the Coliseum for Game Six, on Good Friday, the 13th of April. And it *did* turn out to be a "Good" Friday. The Canucks exploded for four second-period goals — three of them only 2:18 apart — to force a seventh and deciding game back at the Saddledome. The heavily-favoured Flames were now definitely nervous about the tenacious upstarts from the West Coast.

Before a red-clad crowd of 20,062, the Flames jumped out to a 2-1 lead after the first period. Linden tallied on a Canucks power-play early in the second before Calgary went ahead again on a man-advantage of their own. This set the stage for Vancouver defenceman Doug Lidster's first goal of the playoffs which knotted the score at 3-3, and the teams were headed for overtime.

In the extra frame, Canucks had great chances to salt it away as first Petri Skriko came within a whisker of notching the winner; so did Tony Tanti, and then Stan Smyl was foiled on a breakaway by an enormous save by Vernon. Vancouver netminder Kirk McLean was equally brilliant at the other end of the ice. But with just 39 seconds to play in the period, Flames were pressing in the Canuck zone when Jim Peplinski banked a shot towards the slot area where big Joel Otto was standing in front of McLean. The puck bounced off Otto's skate and into the net past the startled Canuck goalie. In 79 minutes and 21 seconds, the netminders had faced 91 shots, 46 by McLean and 45 by Vernon.

Trevor Linden's production dipped a bit in his sophomore season but he remains a solid cornerstone of the Canucks' future.

And even though the Canucks weren't supposed to

advance past, perhaps, four games, they felt robbed by the Flames who, of course, would eventually win the Stanley Cup. Coach McCammon said: "This is Calgary's lucky day. In my heart, I feel the best team is going back to Vancouver." GM Pat Quinn echoed the coach's comments, noting "I couldn't be prouder of these guys. You can't reach down much more than they did."

Canucks' team and individual heroics didn't go unnoticed in the rest of the hockey world that spring. For the first time in club history, the Canucks had three finalists for the NHL's major trophies. Trevor Linden finished second in Calder Trophy voting for Best Rookie; Bob McCammon was runner-up in voting for the Jack Adams Trophy which goes to the Coach-of-the-Year; and Kirk McLean was third in balloting for the Vezina Trophy which goes to the NHL's Outstanding Netminder.

Igor Larionov scored 17 goals and 44 points in his first NHL season. His fine second-half performance indicated that he was a lot more "at home" with the North American game.

1989-90

The excitement and enthusiasm generated by the Canucks' exhilarating finish carried over well into the summer months. More groundwork was laid in June when Vancouver drafted Jason Herter, NHL Central Scouting's top ranked defenceman in the Entry Draft. Also selected was Soviet speedster Pavel Bure, a youngster whose potential had scouts drooling all over the National League. (The selection of Bure was ruled ineligible at first because the League contended that he hadn't played the prescribed number of games. But

Ronnie Stern worked extremely hard to earn a starting position on the Canucks roster in '89-90. The fans loved his rugged style which earned him the Most Aggressive Player Award.

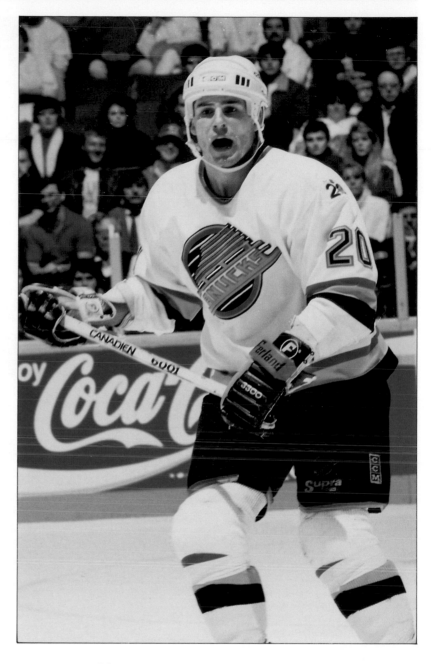

OPPOSITE PAGE:

Brian Bradley was a one-man highlight package in '89-90 as he made one spectacular play after another en route to the best season of his career (19 goals, 29 assists).

provision of further data by Pat Quinn and his staff reinforced their initial faith in his eligibility and NHL President John Ziegler overturned his original ruling just prior to the 1990 draft).

A July 1, 1989 announcement that World Class Soviet centre Igor Larionov had signed a Canuck contract evoked even more interest. This was a landmark day in the history of the Canucks, for it brought to fruition four years of monumental efforts on the part of the Griffiths family (owners of the team), Senator Ray Perrault, a Director of the hockey club, and, of course, Quinn, who finally plucked the Soviet star out of the Soviet Union. Two separate agreements had to be negotiated and numerous trips were made to

Vladimir Krutov had some difficulty adapting to the NHL style but showed flashes of brilliance in his inaugural season with the Canucks.

OPPOSITE PAGE:

Canuck fans got a brief taste of Jyrki Lumme's vast playmaking talent at the end of the '89-90 season. His year-end performance won him the final segment of Molson Cup voting.

the U.S.S.R. before Larionov was granted permission to leave his country and play in the NHL.

The buzz created by Larionov's signing was to produce the most active demonstration of ticket interest since Vancouver joined the NHL in 1970. Season ticket sales went from 6,800 in 1988-89 to 10,300 in '89-90 and crowds averaged 15,400, up from 13,700 the season before.

Another flurry of excitement was created in early September when the Canucks landed Larionov's left winger, Vladimir Krutov.

The Canucks embarked on their 20th National Hockey League season in nifty new togs, too. Precipitated by Pat Quinn, the change was quite dramatic. The Vancouver GM explained at the time: "This move is really the culmination of the evolution of the 'V' style jersey first introduced in 1978-79 and then modified in 1985-86. We've retained the strongest feature of the uniform — namely the dynamic skate logo — while returning to the traditional white field color which characterizes NHL home jerseys."

"Tradition" was the watchword on opening weekend, 1990, as 16 of the original 1970-71 Canucks were brought back to Vancouver to help kick off the 20th season. Many had not been back since that auspicious debut season. On hand were such early luminaries as Andre Boudrias, Charlie Hodge, Bobby Schmautz, Rosaire Paiement, Murray Hall plus, of course, Orland Kurtenbach and Pat Quinn. An entire weekend of festivities, fun and frolic was laid on for the group which revelled in renewing old acquaintances. Canucks' first GM Bud Poile joined the group, as did Malcolm Ashford, one of the linesmen in Canucks' first-ever NHL game.

Later in the year, a very successful promotion was conducted whereby fans were asked to vote for the players they felt belonged on the all-time "Canuck Dream Team." When the results were all tabulated, the team consisted of the following players: Richard Brodeur in goal; Harold Snepsts and Paul Reinhart on defence; Thomas Gradin at centre; Don Lever at left wing and Stan Smyl on right wing. The popular sextet gathered at centre ice at a home game in January where each received a gold watch and a commemorative framed Glen Green painting (depicted on our cover) to celebrate the event. Gradin travelled all the way from Sweden to attend while Brodeur flew in from Quebec and Lever from Buffalo.

As far as the season itself was concerned it was another of frustration. The team got off to its best start ever, going 7-5-1 in October. But that performance flattened out into a 7-27-8 streak over the next several months. And despite a real return to respectability in February and March when they won 11 games, tied five and lost nine (a .540 pace), it was too late to stay in playoff contention.

Along the way, GM Pat Quinn decided that the Canucks needed an injection of new blood that could perhaps shake up the lineup in a positive way. On Jan. 8, 1990, a major trade was announced which brought centre Dan Quinn, right winger Andrew McBain and rookie forward Dave Capuano from Pittsburgh in

Stan Smyl had a frustrating season but came to play every night, displaying the robust style which has been his trademark since entering the NHL.

Big Jim Sandlak is most effective when he throws his weight (220 lbs.) around.

OPPOSITE PAGE:

Dan Quinn came to the Canucks from Pittsburgh halfway through the season and promptly set about winning the team scoring title.

exchange for veterans Barry Pederson, Tony Tanti and the return of defenceman Rod Buskas, obtained from the Penguins in an earlier deal.

Continuing his quest for an improved lineup, Quinn engineered three deals just prior to the March trading deadline. First he acquired defenceman Adrien Plavsic and two draft picks from St. Louis for Rich Sutter and Harold Snepsts. Quinn then traded one of the draft choices received from the Blues to Montreal for defenceman Jyrki Lumme. He concluded the day by acquiring another rearguard, Jack Capuano from the New York Islanders in exchange for minor league centre Jeff Rohlicek.

The transactions paid dividends as Dan Quinn went on to lead the Canucks in scoring the rest of the way

Over 19,000 fans showed up at B.C. Place Stadium for the NHL Entry Draft. It marked the first time the event had ever been staged in Vancouver.

with 16 goals and 18 assists for 34 points in his final 37 games. Lumme became an instant crowd favourite as he collected 10 points in his last 11 games (including an overtime goal which gave Vancouver a 6-5 win over his old teammates in St. Louis).

Meanwhile, Paul Reinhart was again the cornerstone of the Canuck defence corps, scoring 17 goals and adding 40 assists for 57 points. And Greg Adams rebounded from a disappointing 19-goal year to tally 30 goals to lead the team in that department.

As mentioned, all this was insufficient to land the Canucks a playoff spot but it did pave the way to an outstanding draft day when the NHL held its annual event and congress in Vancouver for the first time in league history. Canucks enjoyed the luxury of owning three of the top 23 overall selections (#2, #18 and #23). A labour dispute prevented the team from hosting the

Draft day, 1990...a smiling first-round draft pick, Petr Nedved, is flanked by ex-Canuck Ivan Hlinka and team captain Stan Smyl. Nedved set a rookie record in the Western Hockey League in '89-90 by scoring 65 goals and 80 assists for 145 goals.

Entry Draft at the Pacific Coliseum so it was moved downtown to B.C. Place Stadium. Team management, having decided to open the doors to the public to witness the event free of charge, had no idea how many fans would drop by. They were hoping to surpass the estimated 9,000 that had attended the 1989 draft in Minnesota.

Saturday, June 16 dawned grey and drizzly ... perfect conditions to head indoors. And head indoors, they did. When the last fan clicked through the turnstiles, the final tally was 19,127! And the roar they let out when GM Pat Quinn stepped up to the microphone was thunderous when he announced: "The Canucks are proud to select from the Seattle Thunderbirds and Czechoslovakia, Petr Nedved."

The Canucks at the annual Molson Slo-Pitch Tournament in Niagara Falls didn't win many games but thoroughly enjoyed this "fun" fundraiser.

OPPOSITE PAGE:
Greg and Kim Adams strut their stuff at a Canuck fundraising fashion show.

Nedved, who had left his home and family in Europe eighteen months earlier, leapt to his feet and raised his arms high in the air. The smile, which never left his face for the next two hours, convinced everyone that he was ecstatic to be selected by Vancouver. The 6'3", 180-lb. centre had celebrated his rookie year in the Western Hockey League by smashing the record for points by a freshman with 145, including 65 goals and 80 assists. Universally acknowledged as the "most gifted player available in the 1990 draft," Nedved drew raves from scouts around the NHL who said such things as: "he's going to be a superstar in the NHL ... he makes moves that other 18-year-olds can only dream about ... has the ability to break a game wide open...."

With pick #18, Quinn evoked another huge ovation by choosing gargantuan winger Shawn Antoski from North Bay of the OHL. The imposing 20-year-old — 6'4", 235 lbs. — presented an impressive image as he donned his Canuck jersey alongside Quinn. He was deemed by many veteran observers as "the prospect

111

The late Walter (Babe) Pratt was a Canuck goodwill ambassador from the team's inception in 1970 until his death in December, 1988. His wisdom and humour charmed thousands of B.C. hockey fans over the years.

most ready to play in the NHL right now." He also drew an even wider smile from Nedved who shook hands with Antoski while proclaiming "my friend!", obviously happy to be on the same side.

Quinn rounded out his first three picks by selecting Czech defenceman Jiri Slegr, the son of Former Canuck blueliner Jiri Bubla. Slegr, a member of the Czech Junior National Team, also played for Litvinov, the team in the CSSR coached by another ex-Canuck, Ivan Hlinka. His NHL potential is very real, according to NHL Central Scouting, which calls Slegr "a leader, both on and off the ice."

At the conclusion of the draft, a comment made the rounds that "there wasn't one of the other 20 NHL managers that wouldn't have swapped his first three picks for those selected by the Canucks."

Following the day's proceedings, Quinn noted: "In Petr Nedved, we feel we have the player with the most potential of any available in this draft and who definitely could be the most talented player in the history of the Vancouver franchise. We've increased our overall size, as well, but not at the expense of talent."

"I'd just like to conclude by commending the hockey fans of Vancouver. With over 19,000 on hand at the draft ... with the patience, loyalty and support you've shown over the 20-year history of this franchise ... you've again proved you're the best in the National Hockey League."

Stan Smyl plays waiter to sportscaster Dave Hodge at the annual "Waiter, There's a Puck in My Soup" dinner which raises money for the Canuck Foundation, the hockey club's fundraising arm.

*Message to Canuck Fans from Pat Quinn,
President and General Manager:*

*"I was a proud Canuck back in 1970, and
though I was away for many seasons, the team
has always been a part of me and remains a
powerful source of pride 20 years later.*

*As you've read in this book, the game of hockey
has enjoyed a rich tradition in Vancouver; it long-
preceded me and will endure for years after me
and our current players are gone.*

*But tradition is what builds great teams and
great communities. You fans have upheld a
tradition of loyalty which has endured for two
decades. We cherish that support and are
determined to reward it. Our players, past and
present, know the common bond that exists
between the team and the city of Vancouver.*

*And as we embark on our third decade, we
pledge to you ... perseverance, persistence and
patience ... in achieving our goal: a team of which
you can all be proud ... a winning team ... an
entertaining team.*

*Here's to the next 20 years! May they be
rewarding and memorable!"*

*Pat Quinn
President and General Manager*

114

FOR THE RECORD

CANUCKS' CAREER SCORING (1970-1990)

Rich Sutter brought the same feisty style of play to the Canucks that characterized the entire Sutter clan throughout the rest of the NHL.

Stan (Steamer) Smyl, the Canucks all-time point leader.

	Player	GP	G	A	PTS	PIM
1.	S. Smyl	851	260	399	659	1469
2.	T. Gradin	613	197	353	550	280
3.	T. Tanti	531	250	220	470	489
4.	D. Lever	593	186	221	407	354
5.	A. Boudrias	458	121	267	388	138
6.	P. Skriko	452	167	198	365	213
7.	P. Sundstrom	374	133	209	342	181
8.	D. Kearns	677	31	290	321	386
9.	D. Ververgaert	409	139	165	304	177
10.	C. Oddleifson	469	85	180	265	439
11.	D. Rota	289	120	116	236	453
12.	R. Lanz	417	56	171	227	331
13.	R. Blight	324	96	125	221	168
14.	D. Lidster	451	47	168	215	374
15.	B. Schmautz	285	108	103	211	433
16.	C. Fraser	348	92	114	206	651
17.	K. McCarthy	352	51	148	199	388
18.	B. Pederson	233	60	137	197	174
19.	H. Snepsts	781	35	160	195	1446
20.	G. O'Flaherty	435	98	95	193	166
21.	B. Lalonde	353	72	117	189	185
22.	I. Boldirev	216	80	104	184	105
23.	R. Sedlbauer	325	108	69	177	170
24.	D. Williams	312	83	82	165	1314
25.	O. Kurtenbach	229	62	101	163	200
26.	D. Halward	324	45	118	163	389
27.	M. Lemay	279	70	92	162	367
28.	G. Adams	206	85	74	159	72
29.	J. Gould	218	82	76	158	53
30.	G. Lupul	293	70	75	145	243
31.	G. Monahan	287	58	82	140	166
32.	J. Gillis	319	63	75	138	210
33.	D. Tallon	222	44	93	137	219
34.	J. Sandlak	292	67	67	134	360
35.	J. Guevremont	227	44	88	132	124
36.	B. Dailey	257	38	93	131	417
37.	W. Maki	180	53	70	123	148
38.	I. Hlinka	137	42	81	123	28
39.	R. Sutter	291	61	61	122	533
40.	G. Butcher	541	27	95	122	1411
41.	L. Lindgren	335	23	99	122	292
42.	J. Bubla	256	17	101	118	202
43.	P. Reinhart	131	24	90	114	74
44.	M. Walton	115	44	69	113	71
45.	T. Linden	153	51	59	110	84

Gary Doak

Doug Halward

	Player	GP	G	A	PTS	PIM
46.	C. Neely	201	51	53	104	320
47.	H. Graves	196	42	61	103	49
48.	B. Bradley	149	40	61	101	113
49.	P.O. Brasar	181	37	63	100	21
50.	L. Molin	172	33	65	98	37
51.	R. Paiement	146	44	47	91	269
52.	R. Lemieux	192	29	61	90	68
53.	B. Wilkins	276	21	69	90	458
54.	P. Bordeleau	183	33	56	89	47
55.	S. Tambellini	161	42	45	87	34
56.	M. Petit	226	24	57	81	373
57.	P. Martin	131	27	45	72	60
58.	M. Hall	109	27	44	71	28
59.	J. Benning	241	15	55	70	172
60.	B. Manno	161	13	55	68	115
61.	G. Boddy	273	23	44	67	263
62.	D. Tannahill	111	30	33	63	25
63.	M. Robitaille	174	10	50	60	121
64.	S. Bozek	129	31	27	58	96
65.	M. Corrigan	95	24	32	56	128
66.	P. McNab	88	24	31	55	20
67.	J.J. Daigneault	131	9	46	55	114
68.	B.J. MacDonald	88	26	28	54	32
69.	R. Nordmark	124	8	46	54	131
70.	B. Peterson	146	15	38	53	171
71.	M. Crawford	176	19	31	50	229
72.	T. Taylor	125	20	29	49	141
73.	D. Hodgson	74	16	33	49	52
74.	B. Ashton	124	23	25	48	68
75.	I. Larionov	74	17	27	44	20
76.	N. Belland	106	13	31	44	54
77.	D. Balon	116	22	21	43	43
78.	J. Wright	91	13	30	43	43
79.	D. Bruce	143	23	18	41	245
80.	D. Lowry	165	19	21	40	357
81.	J. Nill	124	17	23	40	219
82.	T. Pratt	176	9	30	39	261
83.	J. Butler	128	18	20	38	96
84.	M. Kirton	119	23	14	37	27
85.	R. Delorme	210	17	20	37	383
86.	B. Gassoff	122	19	17	36	163
87.	A. Demarco	95	13	22	35	18
88.	J. Grisdale	199	3	32	35	266
89.	D. Quinn	37	16	18	34	27
90.	B. Derlago	63	15	19	34	29
91.	W. Connellly	53	14	20	34	12
92.	A. MacAdam	80	14	20	34	27
93.	V. Krutov	61	11	23	34	20
94.	P. Popiel	116	11	23	34	97
95.	R. Cullen	70	12	21	33	42
96.	D. Dunn	69	11	22	33	87
97.	L. Rochefort	87	18	14	32	2
98.	J.M. Lanthier	105	16	16	32	29
99.	G. Minor	140	11	21	32	173

Gary Bromley

	Player	GP	G	A	PTS	PIM
100.	C. Coxe	170	10	21	31	508
101.	D. Johnson	77	16	14	30	16
102.	L. Goodenough	113	7	21	28	75
103.	D. Wickenheiser	80	7	19	26	36
104.	C. Alexander	32	8	18	26	6
105.	G. Meehan	57	10	15	25	4
106.	R. Boyd	62	7	17	24	64
107.	J. McIlhargey	167	6	18	24	403
108.	J. LeBlanc	43	13	10	23	18
109.	D. Richter	127	4	19	23	396
110.	R. Vaive	47	13	8	21	111
111.	L. Melnyk	190	5	16	21	246
112.	B. McSheffrey	87	13	7	20	44
113.	R. Stewart	53	8	12	20	4
114.	D. Saunders	56	7	13	20	10
115.	J. Schella	115	2	18	20	224
116.	P. Quinn	133	4	14	18	212
117.	C. Campbell	89	2	13	17	206
118.	T. Currie	38	9	7	16	4
119.	D. Sanderson	16	7	9	16	30
120.	T. Hall	34	7	9	16	25
121.	M. Marois	50	4	12	16	115
122.	A. Spruce	51	9	6	15	37
123.	D. Stanley	100	6	9	15	192
124.	D. Smith	40	6	8	14	76
125.	W. Huber	35	4	10	14	40
126.	R. Eriksson	35	2	12	14	4
127.	R. Summanen	19	6	7	13	2
128.	B. Murray	90	3	10	13	42
129.	J. Hughes	52	2	11	13	181
130.	A. Schliebener	84	2	11	13	74
131.	G. Doak	82	2	11	13	135
132.	L. Carrière	56	1	12	13	66
133.	I. Kidd	20	4	7	11	25
134.	J. Korab	31	4	7	11	64
135.	K. Guy	75	4	7	11	66
136.	A. Eldebrink	43	2	9	11	21
137.	J. Wiley	37	4	6	10	6
138.	J. Lumme	11	3	7	10	8
139.	A. McBain	26	4	5	9	22
140.	G. Richardson	24	3	6	9	19
141.	R. Tudor	26	4	4	8	19
142.	K. Berry	27	4	4	8	11
143.	D. Capuano	27	3	5	8	10
144.	B. Maxwell	30	1	7	8	28
145.	S. Kannegiesser	42	1	7	8	36
146.	J. Hargreaves	66	1	7	8	105
147.	R. Brodeur (G)	377	0	8	8	24
148.	M. Bridgman	15	4	3	7	10
149.	G. Rizzuto	37	3	4	7	16
150.	D. Kozak	28	2	5	7	30
151.	G.C. Adams	12	4	2	6	35
152.	R. Stern	66	3	3	6	309
153.	J. Mair	23	2	4	6	8

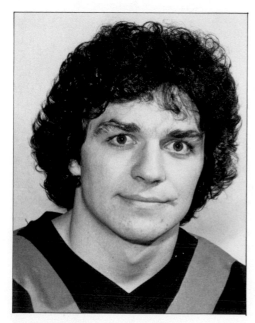

Kevin McCarthy

Ray Cullen

Hilliard Graves

Danny Johnson

	Player	GP	G	A	PTS	PIM
154.	R. Ward	71	2	4	6	4
155.	D. Seguin	26	1	5	6	46
156.	D. Logan	40	1	5	6	122
157.	K. McLean (G)	146	0	6	6	20
158.	A. Plavsic	11	3	2	5	8
159.	B. Wilcox	33	3	2	5	15
160.	D. Callander	21	3	1	4	2
161.	Ron Stewart	42	3	1	4	10
162.	S. Kulak	32	2	2	4	37
163.	L. Lunde	20	1	3	4	2
164.	B. Smith	21	1	3	4	52
165.	R. Holt	22	1	3	4	80
166.	E. Hatoum	26	1	3	4	21
167.	D. Fortier	58	1	3	4	125
168.	K. Manery	21	2	1	3	15
169.	F. Speck	18	1	2	3	0
170.	J. Wiste	23	1	2	3	0
171.	R. Murphy	25	1	2	3	4
172.	R. Flockhart	38	1	2	3	12
173.	M. Stevens	6	0	3	3	6
174.	R. Buskas	17	0	3	3	36
175.	G. Martin	24	0	3	3	45
176.	G. Cochrane	63	0	3	3	177
177.	F. Caprice (G)	102	0	3	3	17
178.	G. Hanlon (G)	137	0	3	3	107
179.	D. Woodley	5	2	0	2	17
180.	P. Bakovic	10	2	0	2	48
181.	C. Vilgrain	6	1	1	2	0
182.	M. Christie	9	1	1	2	0
183.	H. Young	11	0	2	2	25
184.	M. Reaume	27	0	2	2	4
185.	D. Sly	31	0	2	2	10
186.	G. Bromley (G)	73	0	2	2	8
187.	G. Smith (G)	208	0	2	2	104
188.	T. Lenardon	8	1	0	1	4
189.	M. Lampman	13	1	0	1	0
190.	B. Affleck	5	0	1	1	0
191.	G. Hubick	5	0	1	1	0
192.	J. McDonnell	7	0	1	1	12
193.	C. Levie	9	0	1	1	13
194.	J. Charbonneau	13	0	1	1	6
195.	L. Zetterstrom	14	0	1	1	2
196.	J. Agnew	21	0	1	1	52
197.	W. Young	30	0	1	1	0
198.	R. Bartel	40	0	1	1	14
199.	J. Garrett (G)	56	0	1	1	23
200.	C. Maniago (G)	93	0	1	1	18
201.	C. Ridley (G)	96	0	1	1	13
202.	D. Wilson (G)	148	0	1	1	39
203.	M. Bannerman (G)	1	0	0	0	0
204.	K. Block	1	0	0	0	0
205.	D. Dunbar	1	0	0	0	2
206.	S. Hazlett	1	0	0	0	0
207.	R. Homenuke	1	0	0	0	0

Ivan Hlinka

	Player	GP	G	A	PTS	PIM
208.	B. Hurlburt	1	0	0	0	2
209.	B. MacDonald	1	0	0	0	0
210.	G. Sobchuk	1	0	0	0	0
211.	S. Veysey	1	0	0	0	0
212.	B. Cook	2	0	0	0	0
213.	P. Folco	2	0	0	0	0
214.	D. Gloor	2	0	0	0	0
215.	L. Gould	2	0	0	0	0
216.	B. Holloway	2	0	0	0	0
217.	D. McClelland (G)	2	0	0	0	0
218.	K. Primeau	2	0	0	0	0
219.	S. Stone	2	0	0	0	0
220.	R. Heinz (G)	3	0	0	0	0
221.	D. McCord	3	0	0	0	6
222.	P. O'Neill	5	0	0	0	0
223.	T. Gamble	6	0	0	0	0
224.	J. Mazur	6	0	0	0	4
225.	T. Hawkins	8	0	0	0	15
226.	D. Morrison	8	0	0	0	0
227.	J. Rohlicek	9	0	0	0	8
228.	J. Caron (G)	10	0	0	0	2
229.	K. Ellacott (G)	12	0	0	0	0
230.	J. Arbour	13	0	0	0	12
231.	L. Bolonchuk	15	0	0	0	6
232.	B. Bullock (G)	16	0	0	0	2
233.	C. Hodge (G)	35	0	0	0	0
234.	G. Gardner (G)	42	0	0	0	0
235.	E. Dyck (G)	49	0	0	0	0
236.	K. Lockett (G)	55	0	0	0	0
237.	S. Weeks (G)	65	0	0	0	4

There's no name more synonymous with Canuck hockey than Jim Robson's over the club's first two decades in the NHL.

Bill Cunningham, long before he became team photographer.

CANUCKS' CAREER GOALTENDING

	Player	GPI	MINS	GA	SO	AVE.	W	L	T
1.	Richard Brodeur	377	21548	1389	6	3.87	126	172	62
2.	Gary Smith	208	10304	572	11	3.33	72	81	23
3.	Dunc Wilson	148	7919	518	2	3.93	24	86	12
4.	Kirk McLean	146	8596	490	5	3.42	52	74	16
5.	Glen Hanlon	137	7770	461	5	3.56	43	66	21
6.	Frank Caprice	102	5589	391	1	4.20	31	47	11
7.	Curt Ridley	96	5183	328	1	3.80	25	44	16
8.	Cesare Maniago	93	5269	323	2	3.68	27	45	17
9.	Gary Bromley	73	3982	241	3	3.63	25	27	14
10.	Steve Weeks	65	3748	212	0	3.39	19	33	11
11.	John Garrett	56	2994	205	1	4.11	22	21	5
12.	Ken Lockett	55	2348	131	2	3.32	13	15	8
13.	Ed Dyck	49	2353	178	1	4.54	8	28	5
14.	George Gardner	42	2162	138	0	3.83	9	22	4
15.	Charlie Hodge	35	1967	112	0	3.41	15	13	8
16.	Wendell Young	30	1443	96	0	3.99	5	15	4
17.	Bruce Bullock	16	927	74	0	4.79	3	9	3
18.	Ken Ellacott	12	555	41	0	4.43	2	3	4
19.	Jacques Caron	10	465	38	0	4.90	2	5	1
20.	Troy Gamble	6	362	16	0	2.65	2	4	0
21.	Rick Heinz	3	180	9	1	3.00	1	1	0
22.	Dave McClelland	2	120	10	0	5.00	1	1	0
23.	Murray Bannerman	1	20	0	0	0.00	0	0	0

Kirk McLean

1970-71
SEASON FINISH - 6TH IN EAST DIVISION

GP	W	L	T	GF	GA	PTS	PCT.
78	24	46	8	229	296	56	.359

Top ten Canuck scorers

PLAYER	GP	G	A	PTS	PIM
Andre Boudrias	77	25	41	66	16
Wayne Maki	78	25	38	63	99
Rosaire Paiement	78	34	28	62	152
Murray Hall	77	21	38	59	22
Dale Tallon	78	14	42	56	58
O. Kurtenbach	52	21	32	53	84
Mike Corrigan	76	21	28	49	103
Ray Cullen	70	12	21	33	42
Poul Popiel	78	10	22	32	61
Ted Taylor	56	11	16	27	53

The Goalies

	GPI	AVE.	SO	RECORD
George Gardner	18	3.38	0	6-8-1
Charlie Hodge	35	3.41	0	15-13-5
Dunc Wilson	35	4.28	0	3-25-2

For the record
The First Year Canucks were led by "Cracklin Rosie's" 34 goals and the Superpest's 66 points, while Dale Tallon broke Bobby Orr's point mark for rookie defencemen (56).

1971-72
SEASON FINISH - 7TH IN EAST DIVISION

GP	W	L	T	GF	GA	PTS	PCT.
78	20	50	8	203	297	48	.308

Top ten Canuck scorers

PLAYER	GP	G	A	PTS	PIM
Andre Boudrias	78	27	34	61	24
O. Kurtenbach	78	24	37	51	48
J. Guevremont	75	13	38	51	44
Dave Balon	75	23	24	47	23
Wayne Maki	76	22	25	47	43
Wayne Connelly	68	19	25	44	14
Dale Tallon	69	17	27	44	78
Rosaire Paiement	69	10	19	29	117
Dennis Kearns	73	3	26	29	59
Bobby Schmautz	60	12	13	25	82

The Goalies

	GPI	AVE.	SO	RECORD
Dunc Wilson	53	3.61	1	16-30-3
Ed Dyck	12	3.66	0	1-6-2
George Gardner	24	4.17	0	3-14-3

For the record
The Canucks' second NHL campaign featured the only scoreless game in team history, when Dunc Wilson got the team's first ever shutout, in a 0-0 tie at Toronto, Oct. 27, 1971.

1972-73
SEASON FINISH - 7TH IN EAST DIVISION

GP	W	L	T	GF	GA	PTS	PCT.
78	22	47	9	233	339	51	.327

Top ten Canuck scorers

PLAYER	GP	G	A	PTS	PIM
Bobby Schmautz	77	38	33	71	137
Andre Boudrias	77	30	40	70	24
Richard Lemieux	78	17	35	52	41
Bobby Lalonde	77	20	27	47	32
Don Tannahill	78	22	21	43	21
J. Guevremont	78	16	26	42	46
Don Lever	78	12	26	38	49
Dale Tallon	75	13	24	37	83
John Wright	71	10	27	37	37
Dennis Kearns	72	4	33	37	51

The Goalies

	GPI	AVE.	SO	RECORD
Dunc Wilson	43	3.94	1	13-21-5
Ed Dyck	25	4.53	1	5-17-1
Bruce Bullock	14	4.79	0	3-8-3
Dave McLelland	2	5.00	0	1-1-0

For the record
Vancouver was paced by the sniping of winger Bobby Schmautz, who set club marks for goals (38) and points (71). He also had three hat tricks, which included a pair of four-goal games.

1973-74
SEASON FINISH - 7TH IN EAST DIVISION

GP	W	L	T	GF	GA	PTS	PCT.
78	24	43	11	224	296	59	.378

Top ten Canuck scorers

PLAYER	GP	G	A	PTS	PIM
Andre Boudrias	78	16	59	75	18
D. Ververgaert	78	26	31	57	25
Don Lever	78	23	25	48	28
Gerry O'Flaherty	78	22	20	42	18
J. Guevremont	72	15	24	39	34
Dave Dunn	68	11	22	33	76
Barry Wilkins	78	3	28	31	123
Chris Oddleifson	70	13	16	29	44
John Gould	75	13	12	25	10
Paulin Bordeleau	68	11	13	24	20

The Goalies

	GPI	AVE.	SO	RECORD
Gary Smith	65	3.44	3	20-33-8
Ed Dyck	12	4.63	0	2-5-2
Jacques Caron	10	4.90	0	2-5-1

For the record
Dennis Ververgaert establishes a new club standard for goals by a rookie, with 26. Gary Smith becomes the first Canuck netminder to win 20 games in a season and gets three shutouts.

1974-75
SEASON FINISH - 1ST IN SMYTHE DIVISION

GP	W	L	T	GF	GA	PTS	PCT.
80	38	32	10	271	254	86	.538

Top ten Canuck scorers

PLAYER	GP	G	A	PTS	PIM
Andre Boudrias	77	16	62	78	46
Don Lever	80	38	30	68	49
John Gould	78	34	31	65	27
D. Ververgaert	57	19	32	51	25
Chris Oddleifson	60	16	35	51	54
Paulin Bordeleau	67	17	31	48	21
Bob Dailey	70	12	36	48	103
Bobby Lalonde	74	17	30	47	48
Gerry O'Flaherty	80	25	17	42	37
Garry Monahan	79	14	20	34	51

The Goalies

	GPI	AVE.	SO	RECORD
Gary Smith	72	3.09	6	32-24-9
Ken Lockett	25	3.16	2	6-7-1
Bruce Bullock	1	4.00	0	0-1-0

For the record
Vancouver earns a first place finish for only time in team history, with a team record 38 wins and 86 points. In their first ever playoff series, they fall four games to one to Montreal.

1975-76
SEASON FINISH - 2ND IN SMYTHE DIVISION

GP	W	L	T	GF	GA	PTS	PCT.
80	33	32	15	271	272	81	.506

Top ten Canuck scorers

PLAYER	GP	G	A	PTS	PIM
D. Ververgaert	80	37	34	71	53
Don Lever	80	25	40	65	93
Chris Oddleifson	80	16	46	62	88
John Gould	70	32	27	59	16
Rick Blight	74	25	31	56	29
Dennis Kearns	80	5	46	51	48
Bobby Lalonde	71	14	36	50	46
Bob Dailey	67	15	24	39	119
Gerry O'Flaherty	68	20	18	38	47
Andre Boudrias	71	7	31	38	10

The Goalies

	GPI	AVE.	SO	RECORD
Curt Ridley	9	2.28	1	6-0-2
Ken Lockett	30	3.47	0	7-8-7
Gary Smith	51	3.50	2	20-24-6

For the record
Team ties its record for fewest losses in a year (32), enroute to its second best finish ever. The season also has the only penalty-free game in Canuck history, March 13th, vs. NY Rangers.

1976-77
SEASON FINISH - 4TH IN SMYTHE DIVISION

GP	W	L	T	GF	GA	PTS	PCT.
80	25	42	13	235	294	63	.394

Top ten Canuck scorers

PLAYER	GP	G	A	PTS	PIM
Rick Blight	78	28	40	68	32
Dennis Kearns	80	5	55	60	60
Don Lever	80	27	30	57	28
D. Ververgaert	79	27	18	45	38
Garry Monahan	76	18	26	44	48
Hilliard Graves	79	18	25	43	34
Chris Oddleifson	80	14	26	40	81
Ron Sedlbauer	70	18	20	38	29
Derek Sanderson	48	15	22	37	56
Bobby Lalonde	68	17	15	32	39

The Goalies

	GPI	AVE.	SO	RECORD
Cesare Maniago	49	3.36	1	17-21-9
Curt Ridley	37	3.88	0	8-21-4
Bruce Bullock	1	6.67	0	0-0-0

For the record
Sophomore Rick Blight gets four goals in the season opener and goes on to lead the team in goals (28) and points (68). Dennis Kearns sets new records for assists (55) and points (60) by a Canuck defenceman.

1977-78
SEASON FINISH - 3RD IN SMYTHE DIVISION

GP	W	L	T	GF	GA	PTS	PCT.
80	20	43	17	239	320	57	.356

Top ten Canuck scorers

PLAYER	GP	G	A	PTS	PIM
Mike Walton	65	29	37	66	30
Rick Blight	80	25	38	63	33
D. Ververgaert	80	21	33	54	23
Don Lever	75	17	32	49	58
Pit Martin	74	16	32	48	36
Hilliard Graves	80	21	26	47	18
Dennis Kearns	80	4	43	47	27
Jere Gillis	79	23	18	41	35
Chris Oddleifson	78	17	22	39	64
Ron Sedlbauer	62	18	12	30	25

The Goalies

	GPI	AVE.	SO	RECORD
Murray Bannerman	1	0.00	0	0-0-0
Glen Hanlon	4	2.70	0	1-2-1
Cesare Maniago	46	4.02	1	10-24-8
Curt Ridley	40	4.06	0	9-17-8

For the record
Captain Don Lever misses the first game of his NHL career on Jan. 17th, after playing in a club record 437 consecutive contests from the start of his pro career in October, 1972.

1978-79
SEASON FINISH - 2ND IN SMYTHE DIVISION

GP	W	L	T	GF	GA	PTS	PCT.
80	25	42	13	217	291	63	.394

Top ten Canuck scorers

PLAYER	GP	G	A	PTS	PIM
Ron Sedlbauer	79	40	16	56	26
Thomas Gradin	76	20	31	51	22
Don Lever	71	23	21	44	17
Stan Smyl	62	14	24	38	89
Chris Oddleifson	67	11	26	37	51
Curt Fraser	78	16	19	35	116
Dennis Kearns	78	3	31	34	28
Harold Snepsts	76	7	24	31	130
Pit Martin	74	12	14	26	24
Hilliard Graves	62	11	15	26	14

The Goalies

	GPI	AVE.	SO	RECORD
Glen Hanlon	31	3.10	3	12-13-5
Gary Bromley	38	3.81	2	11-19-6
Dunc Wilson	17	4.17	0	2-10-2

For the record
Ron Sedlbauer becomes first Canuck ever to score 40 goals in a year. The Canucks win first game of their playoff series vs. Philadelphia before being knocked out in three games.

1979-80
SEASON FINISH - 3RD IN SMYTHE DIVISION

GP	W	L	T	GF	GA	PTS	PCT.
80	27	37	16	256	281	70	.438

Top ten Canuck scorers

PLAYER	GP	G	A	PTS	PIM
Stan Smyl	77	31	47	78	204
Thomas Gradin	80	30	45	75	22
Ivan Boldirev	79	32	35	67	34
Dave Williams	78	30	23	53	278
Kevin McCarthy	79	15	30	45	70
Curt Fraser	78	17	25	42	143
Lars Lindgren	73	5	30	35	66
Per-Olov Brasar	70	10	24	34	7
Jere Gillis	67	13	17	30	108
Darcy Rota	70	15	14	29	78

The Goalies

	GPI	AVE.	SO	RECORD
Gary Bromley	15	3.00	1	8-2-4
Glen Hanlon	57	3.47	0	17-29-10
Curt Ridley	10	3.91	0	2-6-2

For the record
Stan Smyl is the only player in the NHL in '79-80 to lead his team in goals (31), assists (47), points (78) and penalty minutes (204). Canucks tie club mark for fewest road losses (20).

1980-81
SEASON FINISH - 3RD IN SMYTHE DIVISION

GP	W	L	T	GF	GA	PTS	PCT.
80	28	32	20	289	301	76	.475

Top ten Canuck scorers

PLAYER	GP	G	A	PTS	PIM
Thomas Gradin	79	21	48	69	34
Stan Smyl	80	25	38	63	171
Per-Olov Brasar	80	22	41	63	8
Dave Williams	77	35	27	62	333
Bobby Schmautz	73	27	34	61	137
Ivan Boldirev	72	26	33	59	34
Blair MacDonald	63	24	33	57	37
Darcy Rota	80	25	31	56	124
Kevin McCarthy	80	16	37	53	85
Curt Fraser	77	25	24	49	118

The Goalies

	GPI	AVE.	SO	RECORD
Richard Brodeur	52	3.51	0	17-18-16
Gary Bromley	20	3.80	0	6-6-4
Glen Hanlon	17	4.44	1	5-8-0

For the record
The Canucks finish with a team record eight 20-goal scorers, including Tiger Williams who leads the team with 35 goals and 333 minutes in penalties. Canucks lose playoff series vs. Buffalo 3-0.

1981-82
SEASON FINISH - 2ND IN SMYTHE DIVISION

GP	W	L	T	GF	GA	PTS	PCT.
80	30	33	17	290	286	77	.481

Top ten Canuck scorers

PLAYER	GP	G	A	PTS	PIM
Thomas Gradin	76	37	49	86	32
Stan Smyl	80	34	44	78	144
Ivan Boldirev	78	33	40	73	45
Curt Fraser	79	28	39	67	175
Ivan Hlinka	72	23	37	60	16
Tony Currie	60	23	25	48	19
Lars Molin	72	15	31	46	10
Kevin McCarthy	71	6	39	45	84
Darcy Rota	51	20	20	40	139
Dave Williams	77	17	21	38	341

The Goalies

	GPI	AVE.	SO	RECORD
Rick Heinz	3	3.00	1	2-1-0
Richard Brodeur	52	3.35	2	20-18-12
Glen Hanlon	28	3.95	1	8-14-5

For the record
Vancouver's 77 point season is its third best year ever. The team, paced by Richard Brodeur's 2.70 average in the playoffs, goes on to the Stanley Cup final, losing to the NY Islanders.

1982-83
SEASON FINISH - 3RD IN SMYTHE DIVISION

GP	W	L	T	GF	GA	PTS	PCT.
80	30	35	15	303	309	75	.469

Top ten Canuck scorers

PLAYER	GP	G	A	PTS	PIM
Stan Smyl	74	38	50	88	114
Thomas Gradin	80	32	54	86	61
Darcy Rota	73	42	39	81	88
Ivan Hlinka	65	19	44	63	12
Doug Halward	75	19	33	52	83
Rick Lanz	74	10	38	48	46
Patrik Sundstrom	74	23	23	46	30
Kevin McCarthy	74	12	28	40	88
Lars Molin	58	12	27	39	23
Jiri Bubla	72	2	28	30	59

The Goalies	GPI	AVE.	SO	RECORD
John Garrett	17	3.08	1	7-6-3
Richard Brodeur	58	3.79	0	21-26-8
Ken Ellacott	12	4.43	0	2-3-4
Frank Caprice	1	9.00	0	0-0-0

For the record
Left winger Darcy Rota sets a new single season goal record with 42. His linemate Stan Smyl sets a new point standard (88), while Thomas Gradin also goes over 80 points, with 86.

1983-84
SEASON FINISH - 3RD IN SMYTHE DIVISION

GP	W	L	T	GF	GA	PTS	PCT.
80	32	39	9	306	328	73	.456

Top ten Canuck scorers

PLAYER	GP	G	A	PTS	PIM
Patrik Sundstrom	78	38	53	91	37
Tony Tanti	79	45	41	86	50
Thomas Gradin	75	21	57	78	32
Stan Smyl	80	24	43	67	136
Rick Lanz	79	18	39	57	45
Darcy Rota	59	28	20	48	73
Gary Lupul	69	17	27	44	51
Jiri Bubla	62	6	33	39	43
Peter McNab	65	15	22	37	20
Cam Neely	56	16	15	31	57

The Goalies	GPI	AVE.	SO	RECORD
Frank Caprice	19	3.39	1	8-8-2
Richard Brodeur	36	4.01	1	10-21-5
John Garrett	29	4.10	0	14-10-2

For the record
Canucks score a team record 306 goals in the season, led by the records set by Patrik Sundstrom (91 points) and Tony Tanti (45 goals). Canucks also score 90 power-play goals, including 19 by Tanti and 14 by Rick Lanz.

1984-85
SEASON FINISH - 5TH IN SMYTHE DIVISION

GP	W	L	T	GF	GA	PTS	PCT.
80	25	46	9	284	401	59	.369

Top ten Canuck scorers

PLAYER	GP	G	A	PTS	PIM
Patrik Sundstrom	71	25	43	68	46
Stan Smyl	80	27	37	64	100
Thomas Gradin	76	22	42	64	43
Tony Tanti	68	39	20	59	45
Moe Lemay	74	21	31	52	68
Peter McNab	75	23	25	48	10
Cam Neely	72	21	18	39	137
Petri Skriko	72	21	14	35	10
Al MacAdam	80	14	20	34	27
Doug Halward	71	7	27	34	82

The Goalies	GPI	AVE.	SO	RECORD
Richard Brodeur	51	4.67	0	16-27-6
Frank Caprice	28	4.81	0	8-14-3
John Garrett	10	6.49	0	1-5-0

For the record
Canucks equal their team record by having eight players reach the 20 goal mark during the season. Vancouver also ties NHL mark for most overtime wins in regular season play, earning seven victories in extra time.

1985-86
SEASON FINISH - 4TH IN SMYTHE DIVISION

GP	W	L	T	GF	GA	PTS	PCT.
80	23	44	13	282	333	59	.369

Top ten Canuck scorers

PLAYER	GP	G	A	PTS	PIM
Petri Skriko	80	38	40	78	34
Tony Tanti	77	39	33	72	85
Patrik Sundstrom	79	18	48	66	28
Stan Smyl	73	27	35	62	144
Rick Lanz	75	15	38	53	73
Thomas Gradin	71	14	27	41	34
Cam Neely	73	14	20	34	126
Doug Halward	70	8	25	33	111
Moe Lemay	48	16	15	31	92
Brent Peterson	77	8	23	31	94

The Goalies	GPI	AVE.	SO	RECORD
Wendell Young	22	3.58	0	4-9-3
Richard Brodeur	64	4.07	2	19-31-8
Frank Caprice	7	5.45	0	0-4-2

For the record
Tony Tanti leads team with 39 goals and becomes first Canuck player to record 30+ goals in three consecutive seasons. Sophomore left winger Petri Skriko leads Vancouver with 78 points including 38 goals.

1986-87
SEASON FINISH - 5TH IN SMYTHE DIVISION

GP	W	L	T	GF	GA	PTS	PCT.
80	29	43	8	282	314	66	.413

Top ten Canuck scorers

PLAYER	GP	G	A	PTS	PIM
Tony Tanti	77	41	38	79	84
Barry Pederson	79	24	52	76	50
Petri Skriko	76	33	41	74	44
Patrik Sundstrom	72	29	42	71	40
Doug Lidster	80	12	51	63	40
Stan Smyl	66	20	23	43	84
Rick Sutter	74	20	22	42	113
Steve Tambellini	72	16	20	36	14
Jim Sandlak	78	15	21	36	66
Raimo Summanen	58	14	11	25	15

The Goalies

	GPI	AVE.	SO	RECORD
Richard Brodeur	53	3.59	1	20-25-5
Frank Caprice	25	3.84	0	8-11-2
Troy Gamble	1	4.00	0	0-1-0
Wendell Young	8	4.20	0	1-6-1

For the record
Doug Lidster established a new single season point record for Vancouver defenceman, with 63 points. Team had four 70-point men for the first time.

1987-88
SEASON FINISH - 5TH IN SMYTHE DIVISION

GP	W	L	T	GF	GA	PTS	PCT.
80	25	46	9	272	320	59	.369

Top ten Canuck scorers

PLAYER	GP	G	A	PTS	PIM
Tony Tanti	73	40	37	77	90
Greg Adams	80	36	40	76	30
Barry Pederson	76	19	52	71	92
Petri Skriko	73	30	34	64	32
Stan Smyl	57	12	25	37	110
Doug Lidster	64	4	32	36	105
Jim Benning	77	7	26	33	58
Jim Sandlak	49	16	15	31	81
Rich Sutter	80	15	15	30	165
D. Wickenheiser	80	7	19	26	36

The Goalies

	GPI	AVE.	SO	RECORD
Steve Weeks	9	3.38	0	4-3-2
Kirk McLean	41	3.71	1	11-27-3
Frank Caprice	22	4.18	0	7-10-2
Richard Brodeur	11	4.39	0	3-6-2

For the record
Tony Tanti became only Canuck ever to record 40+ goals in back-to-back seasons. He also scored a club-record 20 power-play tallies in 1987-88.

1988-89
SEASON FINISH - 4TH IN SMYTHE DIVISION

GP	W	L	T	GF	GA	PTS	PCT.
80	33	39	8	251	253	74	.463

Top ten Canuck scorers

PLAYER	GP	G	A	PTS	PIM
Petri Skriko	74	30	36	66	57
Trevor Linden	80	30	29	59	41
Paul Reinhart	64	7	50	57	44
Tony Tanti	77	24	25	49	69
Brian Bradley	71	18	27	45	42
Barry Pederson	62	15	26	41	22
Robert Nordmark	80	6	35	41	97
Jim Sandlak	72	20	20	40	99
Steve Bozek	71	17	18	35	64
Greg Adams	61	19	14	33	24

The Goalies

	GPI	AVE.	SO	RECORD
Troy Gamble	5	2.38	0	2-3-0
Steve Weeks	35	2.98	0	11-19-5
Kirk McLean	42	3.08	4	20-17-3

For the record
Trevor Linden became the first Canuck ever to score 30 goals in his rookie year, finishing runner-up in voting for the Calder Trophy.

1989-90
SEASON FINISH - 5TH IN SMYTHE DIVISION

GP	W	L	T	GF	GA	PTS	PCT.
80	25	41	14	245	306	64	.400

Top ten Canuck scorers

PLAYER	GP	G	A	PTS	PIM
Dan Quinn	78	25	38	63	49
Paul Reinhart	67	17	40	57	30
Trevor Linden	73	21	30	51	43
Greg Adams	65	30	20	50	18
Brian Bradley	67	19	29	48	65
Petri Skriko	77	15	33	48	36
Igor Larionov	74	17	27	44	20
Doug Lidster	80	8	28	36	36
Vladimir Krutov	61	11	23	34	20
Jyrki Lumme	65	4	26	30	49

The Goalies

	GPI	AVE.	SO	RECORD
Kirk McLean	63	3.47	0	21-30-1
Steve Weeks	21	4.15	0	4-11-4

For the record
Three Canuck rookies made their first career NHL goals count, as Vladimir Krutov, Dave Capuano and Rob Murphy all scored game-winning goals with their first NHL tallies.

THEY WORE THE CANUCK COLOURS

1   Kirk McLean (1987-90), Wendell Young (1985-87), Ken Ellacott (1982-83), Glen Hanlon (1978-82), Murray Bannerman (1978), Bruce Bullock (1972-76), Gary Smith (1973-76), Ed Dyck (1971-74), Dunc Wilson (1970-73, 1978-79), George Gardner (1970-72), Charlie Hodge (1970-71)

2   Kevan Guy (1988-90), Ian Kidd (1987-89), Willie Huber (1987-88), Craig Levie (1987), Jim Agnew (1986-89), Doug Halward (1981-86), Bob Manno (1976-81), Dave Logan (1979-80), Lars Zetterstrom (1978-79), Mike Robitaille (1974-77), Jocelyn Guevrement (1971-74), Gary Doak (1970-71)

3   Doug Lidster (1984-90), Michel Petit (1982-87), Garth Butcher (1982-90), Anders Eldebrink (1981-83), Joe McDonnell (1982), Lars Lindgren (1978-83), Bob Dailey (1973-77), Larry Bolochuk (1972), Pat Quinn (1970-72)

4   Jim Benning (1986-90), Rick Lanz (1980-86), John Hughes (1979-80), Randy Holt (1978), Mike Walton (1976-78), Ab Demarco (1974-75), Barry Wilkins (1970-74)

5   Garth Butcher (1982-90), Colin Campbell (1980-82), Gerry Minor (1979-83), Larry Goodenough (1977-80), Brad Smith (1978-80), Larry Carriere (1976-77), Sheldon Kannegiesser (1977-78), Dave Fortier (1976-77), Bob Manno (1976-81), Tracy Pratt (1973-76), Jim Hargreaves (1970-73), John Schella (1971-72), John Arbour (1970), Darryl Sly (1970-71)

6   Robert Nordmark (1988-90), Dave Richter (1986-88), Andy Schliebener (1982-84), Blair MacDonald (1981-83), Dennis Kearns (1971-81), Howie Young (1970-71), Marc Reaume (1970-71)

7   Dan Quinn (1990), Barry Pederson (1986-89), Gary Lupul (1979-86), Tony Currie (1982-84), Gerry Minor (1979-83), Pit Martin (1977-79), Sid Veysey (1977), Dave Fortier (1976-77), Andre Boudrias (1970-76)

8   Greg Adams (1987-90), Taylor Hall (1984-86), Peter McNab (1984-85), Jim Nill (1982-84), Moe Lemay (1982-87), Bobby Schmautz (1971-74, 80-81), Rick Blight (1975-81), Gerry Meehan (1974-75), Wayne Connelly (1971-72), Danny Johnson (1970-71)

9   Andrew McBain (1990), Tony Tanti (1983-90), Ivan Boldirev (1980-83), Don Lever (1972-80), Dale Tallon (1970-73), Bobby Schmautz (1971-74, 80-81), Ed Hatoum (1970-71), Jim Wiste (1970)

10   Brian Bradley (1988-90), Ronnie Stern (1987-90), Brent Peterson (1985-87), Jere Gillis (1977-80, 1983-85), Jean-Marc Lanthier (1984-87), Dave Morrison (1984), Moe Lemay (1982-87), Tony Tanti (1983-90), Tony Currie (1982-84), Anders Eldebrink (1981-83), Rick Blight (1975-81), Drew Callander (1979-80), Billy Derlago (1978-80), Dennis Ververgaert (1973-78), Don Lever (1972-80), Bobby Schmautz (1971-74, 80-81), Fred Speck (1971), Ray Cullen (1970-71)

11   Chris Oddleifson (1974-80), Wayne Maki (1970-72)

12   Stan Smyl (1978-90), Rob Flockhart (1976-79), Jim Wiley (1974-77), Leon Rochefort (1974-76), Danny Gloor (1974), Barry Wilcox (1972-75), Ron Stewart (1971-72), Mike Corrigan (1970-71)

13   Lars Lindgren (1978-83)

14   Steve Bozek (1988-90), Doug Wickenheiser (1987-88), Raimo Summanen (1987-88), Moe Lemay (1982-87), Tony Tanti (1983-90), Blair MacDonald (1981-83), Jere Gillis (1977-80, 83-85), Chris Oddleifson (1974-80), Dennis McCord (1974), Peter Folco (1974), Steve Stone (1974), Danny Seguin (1970-73), John Wright (1972-73), Bobby Schmautz (1970-74, 80-81), Bob Cook (1971), Jim Wiste (1970)

15   Adrien Plavsic (1990), Rich Sutter (1986-90), J.J. Daigneault (1984-86), Neil Belland (1982-85), Brent Ashton (1979-81), Hilliard Graves (1976-79), Paulin Bordeleau (1973-76), Rosaire Paiement (1970-72)

16   Trevor Linden (1988-90), Dan Hodgson (1986-89), Stu Kulak (1982-86), Mark Kirton (1983-85), Per-Olov Brasar (1979-82), Brad Gassoff (1975-79), Len Rochefort (1974-76), Glen Richardson (1976-76), Barry Wilcox (1974-75), Jim Wiley (1974-77), Don Tannahill (1972-74), Ted Taylor (1970-72)

17   Vladimir Krutov (1989-90), Jose Charbonneau (1989), Todd Hawkins (1988-90), Paul Lawless (1988), Rob Murphy (1988-90), Jeff Rohlicek (1987-89), Doug Wickenheiser (1987-88), Patrik Sundstrom (1982-87), Tony Currie (1982-84), Jerry Butler (1980-82), Ron Sedlbauer (1974-79), Drew Callander (1979-80), Larry Gould (1974), Paul O'Neil (1973), John Wright (1972-73),

Ron Ward (1970-72), Danny Seguin (1970-73), Howie Young (1970-71)

18   Igor Larionov (1989-90), Ken Berry (1988-89), Marc Crawford (1981-87), Darcy Rota (1980-84), Brad Smith (1978-80), Rick Vaive (1979-80), Rob Flockhart (1976-79), John Grisdale (1974-79), Jim Mair (1973-75), Larry Gould (1974), Mike Lampman (1973-74), Ron Homenuke (1972), Poul Popiel (1970-72)

19   Jim Sandlak (1985-90), Dale Dunbar (1986), Ron Delorme (1981-84), Mario Marois (1980-81), Rob Tudor (1978-80), Kris Manery (1980), Greg Hubick (1980), Steve Hazlett (1980), Roland Eriksson (1978-79), Claire Alexander (1978), Derek Sanderson (1977), Glen Richardson (1975-76), Jim Wiley (1975-77), Richard Lemieux (1971-74), Ron Stewart (1971-72), Dale Tallon (1970-73)

20   Ronnie Stern (1987-90), Steve Tambellini (1985-88), Grant Martin (1983-84), Gerry Minor (1979-83), John Hughes (1979-80), Drew Callander (1979-80), Bill Delargo (1978-80), Bobby Lalonde (1971-77), George Gardner (1970-72), Jim Hargreaves (1970-73)

21   Jyrki Lumme (1990), Doug Smith (1989-90), Rob Murphy (1988-90), Peter Bakovic (1988), Craig Coxe (1984-90), Cam Neely (1983-86), Ivan Hlinka (1981-83), Doug Halward (1981-86), Jere Gillis (1977-80, 1983-85), John Gould (1973-76), Gene Sobchuk (1973), Dave Balon (1971-73), Dennis Kearns (1971-81), John Arbour (1970)

22   Craig Coxe (1989-90), Greg C. Adams (1989), Dan Hodgson (1986-89), Dave Lowry (1985-88), Tiger Williams (1980-84), Bob Manno (1976-81), Andy Spruce (1977), Greg Boddy (1971-76), Jocelyn Guevrement (1971-74), Garth Rizzuto (1970-71)

23   Paul Reinhart (1988-90), Dan Woodley (1987), Dan Hodgson (1986-89), Thomas Gradin (1978-86), Gerry O'Flaherty (1972-78), Murray Hall (1970-72)

24   Larry Melnyk (1987-90), Michel Petit (1982-87), Doug Lidster (1984-90), Tony Currie (1982-84), Curt Fraser (1978-83), Garry Monahan (1974-78), Dave Dunn (1973-74), Bryan McSheffrey (1972-73), Bruce Bullock (1972-76), Ed Dyck (1971-73), Ralph Stewart (1971, 1976-77), Len Lunde (1970)

25   David Bruce (1986-89), Al MacAdam (1984-85), Doug Lidster (1984-90), Kevin McCarthy (1978-84), Rob Tudor (1978-80), Ralph Stewart (1971, 1986-87), Jim Mair (1973-75), Orland Kurtenbach (1970-74)

26   Petri Skriko (1984-90), Lars Molin (1981-84), Tiger Williams (1980-84), Bruce Affleck (1979), Don Kozak (1979), Ralph Stewart (1971, 1976-77), Bob Murray (1975-77), Gerry Meehan (1974-75), Bob Hurlbut (1974), Steve Stone (1974), Bryan McSheffrey (1972-73), Ken Block (1971), George Gardner (1970-72)

27   Harold Snepsts (1974-84, 1988-90), Randy Boyd (1987-88), John LeBlanc (1987-88), Glen Cochrane (1985-87), Brad Maxwell (1986-87), Craig Coxe (1984-90), Jerry Korab (1973-74)

28   Dave Capuano (1990), Rod Buskas (1989), Mel Bridgman (1989), John LeBlanc (1987-88), Jean-Marc Lanthier (1984-87), Taylor Hall (1984-86), Marc Crawford (1981-87), Colin Campbell (1980-82), Mike Christie (1980-81), Jerry Butler (1980-82), Rick Vaive (1979-80), Larry Goodenough (1977-80), Rob Flockhart (1976-79)

29   Daryl Stanley (1987-90), Randy Boyd (1987-88), Glen Cochrane (1985-87), Jiri Bubla (1981-86), Kevin Primeau (1980), Kris Manery (1980), Jack McIlhargey (1977-79)

30   Frank Caprice (1983-88), Gary Bromley (1978-81), Cesare Maniago (1976-78), Ken Lockett (1974-76), Jacques Caron (1973-74), Ed Dyck (1971-74), Dave McClelland (1973), Bruce Bullock (1972-76), Dunc Wilson (1970-73, 78-79), George Gardner (1970-72)

31   Steve Weeks (1988-90), Troy Gamble (1986-89), John Garrett (1983-85), Rick Heinz (1982), Bruce Bullock (1972-76), Dunc Wilson (1970-73, 78-79)

32   Ian Kidd (1987-89), Jim Agnew (1986-90), Peter Bakovic (1988), Robin Bartel (1986-87), Craig Coxe (1984-90), Bruce Holloway (1985), Neil Belland (1982-85)

33   Jay Mazur (1989-90), David Saunders (1987-88), Jim Sandlak (1985-90), Mike Stevens (1985)

34   Jeff Rohlicek (1987-89), Brett MacDonald (1988), Claude Vilgrain (1988), Ian Kidd (1987-89), Neil Belland (1982-85)

35   Troy Gamble (1986-89), Richard Brodeur (1980-88), Curt Ridley (1976-79), Bruce Bullock (1972-76), Ed Dyck (1971-74)

36   Jim Agnew (1986-90)

38   Todd Hawkins (1988-90)

44   Rob Murphy (1988-90)